HOW TO
TEACH
YOUR BABY
MATH

HOW TO TEACH YOUR BABY MATH

MORE
GENTLE
REVOLUTION

by Glenn Doman
Janet Doman

The Gentle Revolution Press™

Towson, Maryland

Second edition, fourth printing (with Revised Appendix)

Cover photographer: Stan Schnier
Printer: Paragon Press, Honesdale, PA

Cataloging in Publication Data

Doman, Glenn J.
Doman, Janet J.
        How to teach your baby math: more gentle revolution/
        Glenn Doman, Janet Doman.
        p. cm.— (The gentle revolution series)
        Includes index.
        ISBN 1-59117-001-X (hard)
        ISBN 1-59117-002-8 (pbk.)

1. Mathematics—Study and teaching (Preschool) 2. Infants I. Title

Table of Contents

This book is dedicated with understanding to all of us who ever wondered *why* you put down the two and carried the seven.

It is offered in comradeship to all of us who had arithmetic teachers who were bigger than we were.

It is offered in total empathy with all of us who didn't really *like* math in school, who still don't really *understand* math, and who are still not very confident in adding up the grocery list.

It is offered in brotherhood to all of us who were ever puzzled as to how four dollars' worth of plastic called a calculator can do things that we—with our incredible brains—have not been able to do.

In short—this book is dedicated to almost everybody alive—who is more than two years old.

With a little bit of luck—and some attention to our babies—we'll be the last of the lot.

Introduction

Dear Parents,

Very few people buy a book for the purpose of disagreeing with it.

The fact that you've bought this book means that, no matter how improbable the title sounds, you've got a healthy suspicion that it is possible to teach your baby how to do math, and in that suspicion you are entirely correct.

Indeed you can, and with a degree of success that even you as parents could not have dreamed to be possible.

It will help you to understand how simply this can be done as well as how incredibly far you can take your baby in math, and the great joy that both you and your baby will know in doing it, if you understand the way in which it all came about.

The staff of The Institutes for the Achievement of Human Potential have had a glorious love affair going with mothers for the last thirty-five years. As the director of The Institutes, I must say it has been a great affair, altogether rewarding and fulfilling.

The affair began poorly and was actually forced upon both the parents and us as a sort of blind date. Mutual trust was low and suspicion was high. It would never have happened in the first place if it hadn't been for the hurt kids and their staggering needs. It was their need that forced parents and us into each other's arms.

In the 1940s the parents of severely brain-injured children had no reason to be grateful to professional people and little reason to trust them. In those days the professional people believed that merely to talk of making a brain-injured child well was not only the worst kind of foolishness but that to do so, even as an objective, was somehow deeply immoral. Many professional people still so believe.

We, as professional people who were daily confronted with children who were paralyzed, speechless, blind, deaf, incontinent, and who were universally considered to be hopelessly "mentally retarded," harbored deep suspicion of parents. Even our own early group that was to become the staff of The Institutes for the Achievement of Human Potential began with the unspoken but common professional belief that "all mothers are idiots and that they have no truth in them." This myth, which is still prevalent, has the tragic result that nobody talks to mothers, and the good Lord knows that nobody listens to them.

Beginning with that belief, as we did, it took us several years to learn that mothers, closely followed by fathers, know more about their own children than anybody else alive.

Myths die hard and the process of unlearning is a great deal harder than the process of learning, and for some people, unlearning is simply impossible. It is frightening for me to admit that if the staggering needs of the brain-injured children hadn't forced us into daily nose-to-nose contact with their parents, we would never have learned the truly extraordinary love that parents have for their children, the profound depth of appreciation they have for their children's potential abilities, and the seemingly miraculous accomplishments they can make possible for their children when they understand the very practical way in which the human brain works.

Suspicion dies slowly and true love must be earned. Often, necessity is not only the mother of invention but also the basis for the beginning of love and understanding if neither party can afford the luxury of running away.

Since the brain-injured children needed help desperately, we and the parents were forced into each other's arms in a marriage not merely of convenience but of necessity.

If the hurt children were to have any sort of life worth living it quickly became apparent that both we and their parents were going to have to devote every moment of our lives to bringing this about.

And so we did.

Beginning a project in clinical research is like getting on a train about which we know little. It's a venture full of mystery and excitement, for you do not know whether you'll have a compartment to yourself or be going second class, whether the train has a dining car or not, what the trip will cost or whether you will end up where you had hoped to go or in a foreign place you never dreamed of visiting.

When our team members got on this train at the various stations, we were hoping that our destination was better treatment for severely brain-injured children. None of us dreamed that if we achieved this goal we would stay on the train till we reached a place where brain-injured children might even be made superior to unhurt children.

The trip has thus far taken thirty-five years, the accommodation was second class, and the dining car served mostly sandwiches, night after night, often at three in the morning. The tickets cost all we had, some of us did not live long enough to finish the trip—and none of us would have missed it for anything else the world has to offer. It's been a fascinating trip.

The original passenger list included a brain surgeon, a physiatrist (an M.D. who specializes in physical medicine and rehabilitation), a physical therapist, a speech therapist, a psychologist, an educator and a nurse. Now there are more than a hundred of us all told, with many additional kinds of specialists.

The little team was formed originally because

each of us was individually charged with some phase of the treatment of severely brain-injured children—and each of us individually was failing.

If you are going to choose a creative field in which to work, it is difficult to pick one with more room for improvement than one in which failure has been 100 percent and success is nonexistent.

When we began our work together thirty-five years ago *we had never seen or heard of a single brain-injured child who had ever gotten well.*

The group that formed after our individual failures would today be called a rehabilitation team. In those days so long ago neither of those words was fashionable and we looked upon ourselves as nothing as grand as all that. Perhaps we saw ourselves more pathetically and more clearly as a group who had banded together, much as a convoy does, hoping that we would be stronger together than we had proved to be separately.

We discovered that it mattered very little (except from a research point of view) whether a child had incurred his injury prenatally, at the instant of birth or postnatally. This was rather like being concerned about whether a child had been hit by an automobile before noon, at noon or after noon. What really mattered was which part of his brain had been hurt, how much it had been hurt, and what might be done about it.

We discovered further that it mattered very little whether a child's good brain had been hurt because his parents had incompatible Rh factors, because his mother had an infectious disease such as German measles during the first three months of pregnancy, because there had been an insufficiency of oxygen reaching his brain during the prenatal period, or because he had been born prematurely. The brain can also be hurt as a result of protracted labor, of a fall on the head which causes blood clots on the brain, of a high temperature with encephalitis, of being struck by an automobile, or of a hundred other factors.

Again, while this was significant from the research point of view, it was rather like worrying about whether a particular child had been hit by a car or a hammer. The important thing here was which part of the child's brain was hurt, how much it was hurt, and what we were going to do about it.

In those early days, the world that dealt with brain-injured children held the view that the problems of these children might be solved by treating the symptoms that existed in the ears, eyes, nose, mouth, chest, shoulders, elbows, wrists, fingers, hips, knees, ankles and toes. A large portion of the world still believes this today.

Such an approach did not work then and could not possibly ever work.

Because of this total lack of success, we concluded that if we were to solve the multiple symptoms of the brain-injured child we would have to attack the source of the problem and approach the human brain itself.

While at first this seemed an impossible or at least monumental task, in the years that followed, we and others found both surgical and nonsurgical methods of treating the brain.

First we tackled the problem from a nonsurgical

standpoint. In the years that followed, we became persuaded that if we could not hope to succeed with the dead brain cells, we would have to find ways to reproduce in some manner the neurological growth-patterns of a normal child. This meant understanding how a normal child's brain begins, grows and matures. We studied intently many hundreds of normal newborn babies, infants and children.

As we learned what normal brain growth is and means, we began to find that the simple and long-known basic activities of normal children, such as crawling and creeping, are of the greatest possible importance to the brain. We learned that if such activities are denied to normal children, because of cultural, environmental or social factors, the potential of these children is severely limited. The potential of brain-injured children is even more affected.

As we learned more about ways to reproduce this normal physical pattern of growing up we began to see brain-injured children improve—very, very slightly.

It was about this time, after working for several years with the parents, that our mutual suspicions disappeared. Love and trust were dawning. So thoroughly had we begun to trust our parents' love and innate good sense that we stopped treating the children ourselves and taught the parents *all* we had learned about the brain, laid out programs for the children, and sent the parents home to carry them out. Results got better, rather than declining. Our respect for parents rose considerably.

It was also at about this time that the neurosurgical components of our team began to prove conclusively that the answer lay in the brain itself, by developing successful surgical approaches to it.

A single startling method will serve as an example of the many types of successful brain surgery which are in use today to solve the problems of the brain-injured child.

There are actually two brains, a right brain and a left brain. These two brains are divided right down the middle of the head from front to rear. In well human beings the right brain (or, if you like, the right half of the brain) is responsible for controlling the left side of the body, while the left half of the brain is responsible for running the right side.

If one half of the brain is hurt to any large degree, the results are catastrophic. The opposite side of the body will be paralyzed, and the child will be severely restricted in all functions. Many such children have constant and severe convulsive seizures that do not respond to any known medication.

It need hardly be said that such children also die.

The ancient cry of those who stood for doing nothing had been chanted over and over for decades. That cry was that when a brain cell was dead it was dead and nothing could be done for children with dead brain cells, so don't try. But by 1955 the neurosurgical members of our group were performing an almost unbelievable kind of surgery on such children; it is called hemispherectomy.

Hemispherectomy is precisely what that name implies—the surgical removal of half the human brain.

Now we saw children with half a brain in the

head and with the other half, billions of brain cells, in a jar at the hospital—dead and gone. But the children were not dead.

Instead we saw children with only half a brain who walked, talked and went to school like other children. *Several such children were above average, and at least one of them had an I.Q. in the genius area.*

It was now obvious that if one half of a child's brain was seriously hurt, it mattered little how good the other half was as long as the hurt half remained. If, for example, such a child was suffering convulsions caused by the injured left brain, he would be unable to demonstrate his intelligence until that half was removed in order to let the intact right brain take over the entire function without interference.

We had long held that, contrary to popular belief, a child might have ten dead brain cells and we would not even know it. Perhaps, we said, he might have a hundred dead brain cells and we would not be aware of it. Perhaps, we said, even a thousand.

Not in our wildest dreams had we dared to believe that a child might have *billions* of dead brain cells and yet perform almost as well as and sometimes even better than an average child.

Now the reader must join us in a speculation. How long could we look at Johnny, who had half his brain removed, and see him perform as well as Billy, who had an intact brain, without asking the question, What is wrong with *Billy?* Why did not Billy, who had twice as much brain as Johnny, perform twice as well or at least better?

Having seen this happen over and over again, we began to look with new and questioning eyes at average children.

Were average children doing as well as they might?

Here was an important question we had never dreamed of asking.

In the meantime, the nonsurgical elements of the team had acquired a great deal more knowledge of how such children grow and how their brains develop. As our knowledge of normality increased, our simple methods for reproducing that normality in brain-injured children kept pace. By now we were beginning to see a small number of brain-injured children reach normality by the use of the simple nonsurgical methods of treatment which were steadily evolving and improving.

It is not the purpose of this book to detail either the concepts or the methods used to solve the multiple problems of brain-injured children. Other books, already published or at present in manuscript form, deal with the treatment of the brain-injured child. However, that such problems are being solved daily is of significance in understanding the pathway that led to the knowledge that normal children can perform infinitely better than they are doing at present. It is sufficient to say that extremely simple techniques were devised to reproduce in brain-injured children the patterns of normal development.

As an example, when a brain-injured child is unable to move correctly he is simply taken in an orderly progression through the stages of growth which occur in normal children. First he is helped to move his arms and legs, then to crawl, then to creep, then finally to walk. He is physically aided in doing these things in a patterned sequence. He progresses through these ever higher stages in the same manner as a child does in the grades at school and is given unlimited opportunity to utilize these activities.

A program of this kind having been initiated, we soon began to see severely brain-injured children whose performance rivaled that of children who had not suffered a brain injury. And as the techniques improved even more, we began to see brain-injured children emerge who could not only perform as well as average children but, indeed, who could not be distinguished from them.

As our understanding of neurological growth and normality began to assume a really clear pattern, and as our nonsurgical methods for the recapitulation of normality multiplied, *we even began to see some brain-injured children who performed at above-average, or even superior, levels,* without surgery.

It was exciting beyond measure. It was even a little bit frightening. It seemed clear that we had, at the very least, underestimated every child's potential.

This raised a fascinating question. Suppose we looked at three equally performing seven-year-olds: Albert, half of whose brain was in a jar; Billy, who had a perfectly normal brain; and Charley, who had been treated nonsurgically and who now performed in a totally normal way although there were still millions of dead cells in his brain.

What was wrong with nice, average, unhurt Billy?

What was wrong with *well* children?

Although we were by now working seven-day weeks and eighteen-hour days, each day and hour charged with excitement, we were not doing so alone. So also were the parents, whose own excitement came from the unbelievable things that their hurt children were doing. The love affair had, by the early sixties, produced many hurt children who were totally well in every way and several who were superior. They had become so at home. The love affair worked both ways and had now reached a peak from which it would never fall. What indeed was wrong with well children?

For years our work had been charged with the vibrancy that one feels prior to important events and great discoveries. Through the years the all-enveloping fog of mystery which surrounded our brain-injured children had gradually been dissipated. We had also begun to see other facts for which we had not bargained. These were facts about well children. A logical connection had emerged between the brain-injured (and therefore neurologically dysorganized) child and the well (and therefore neurologically organized) child, where earlier there were only disconnected and disassociated facts about well children. This logical sequence, as it emerged, had pointed insistently to a path by which we might markedly change man himself—and for the better. Was the neurological organization displayed by an average child necessarily the end of the path?

Now, with brain-injured children performing as well as, or better than, average children, the possibility that the path extended further could be fully seen.

It had always been assumed that neurological growth and its end product, ability, were a static and irrevocable fact: this child was capable and that child was not.

Nothing could be further from the truth.

The fact is that neurological growth, which we had always considered a static and irrevocable fact, is a dynamic and ever-changing process.

In the severely brain-injured child we see the process of neurological growth totally halted.

In the "retarded" child we see this process considerably slowed. In the average child it takes place at an average rate, and in the superior child, at above-average speed. We had now come to realize that the brain-injured child, the average child and the superior child are not three different kinds of children but rather represent a continuum ranging from the extreme neurological dysorganization that severe brain injury creates, through the more moderate neurological dysorganization caused by mild or moderate brain injury, through the average amount of neurological organization that the average child demonstrates, to the high degree of neurological organization that a superior child invariably demonstrates.

In the severely brain-injured child we had succeeded in restarting this process, which had come to a halt, and in the retarded child we had accelerated it. It had become clear that the process of neurological growth could be speeded as well as delayed.

Having repeatedly brought brain-injured children from neurological dysorganization to neurological organization of an average or even superior level by employing the simple nonsurgical techniques that had been developed, there was every reason to believe that these same techniques could be used to increase the amount of neurological organization demonstrated by average children. One of these techniques is the teaching of very small brain-injured children to read.

Nowhere is the ability to raise neurological organization more clearly demonstrated than when you teach a well baby to read.

By 1963 there were hundreds of severely brain-injured children who could read and read well, with total understanding at two years of age. They had been taught to do so by their parents at home. Some of the parents had also taught their own well tiny children to do so.

We were ready and had all the information we needed to talk to mothers of well children, and so we did.

In May 1963 we wrote an article called "You Can Teach Your Baby to Read" for the *Ladies' Home Journal*. Letters poured in by the hundreds from mothers who had taught their babies to read successfully and who had found great joy in the doing.

In May of 1964 we published a book called *How to Teach Your Baby to Read;* it was subtitled "The Gentle Revolution." It was published in the United States by Random House and in Britain by Jonathan Cape. Today that book is in fifteen languages. The

letters from mothers have continued to come in—
by the thousands—and they still do.

Those letters report three things over and over
again:

1. That it is much easier to teach a one- or two-
year-old child to read than it is to teach a four-year-
old; and easier to teach a four-year-old than to teach
a seven-year-old.

2. That teaching a tiny child to read brings great
happiness to both mother and baby.

3. That when a tiny child learns to read, not only
does his knowledge grow by leaps and bounds, but
so also does his curiosity and alertness—in short,
that he clearly becomes more intelligent.

The mothers also posed exciting new questions
for us to answer, and high among these questions
was, Now that I've taught my two-year-old to read,
shouldn't it be even easier to teach him math, and if
so, how do I go about doing it?

It took us ten long years to answer this question.
At long last we've answered it and taught hundreds
of tiny well kids and hurt kids to do math easily and
with a degree of success that initially left us in
open-mouthed astonishment. Now it is clearly our
job to make that information available to every
mother alive so that each can decide whether or not
she wishes to take the opportunity to teach her own
baby to do math. This book is our way of informing
mothers that it can be done and how to do it.

And so you see, however improbable it sounds,
your suspicion that you can teach babies to do math
has a very firm foundation in fact.

High on the list of things that we ourselves have

learned is that mothers are, by a long shot, the most superb teachers of children this old world has ever seen.

Have a lovely, loving, and exciting time.

Glenn Doman

P.S. There are no chauvinists at The Institutes, either male or female. We love and respect both mothers and fathers, baby boys and baby girls. To solve the maddening problem of referring to all human beings as "persons" or "tiny persons" we have decided in this manuscript to refer to all parents as mothers and all children as boys. Seems fair.

It will be helpful to the reader in understanding that tiny children are learning math if he understands, at least in a sketchy way, how The Institutes operate.

The Institutes for the Achievement of Human Potential are a group of seven Institutes which exist on the same campus in suburban Philadelphia. Three of these Institutes actually deal with children, while the remaining four are all scientific support Institutes or teaching Institutes for professionals or parents.

Of the three dealing with children, the Institute for the Achievement of Physiological Excellence is the oldest, and deals entirely with brain-injured children, designing programs and teaching their parents how to carry these out at home. The Institute for Human Development is for young adults with severe learning problems.

The third, The Evan Thomas Institute, is for teaching new mothers how to teach their babies to read, do math and do a great many other things, and actually developed as a result of what had been done over past years in the other Institutes.

All three of these Institutes have as their objectives raising these infants, children and young adults to physical, intellectual and social excellence.

1
Mothers and Tiny Kids—
The World's Most
Dynamic Learning Teams

> We mothers are the potters and
> our children the clay.
>
> —Winifred Sackville Stoner
> *Natural Education*

I begin my day, as do most people, with breakfast, which is pleasant, and my daily dose of depression —the morning paper—which is not. Sometimes, as it recites its litany of horror, of war, of murder, of rape, of cruelty, of insanity, of death and of destruction I put it aside with the feeling that there isn't going to be any tomorrow and if this proves to be the case, then that just might be the best piece of news of all. But the morning paper is one form of reality; happily, it is not the only form. And I have a guaranteed way of putting the world back into instant and delightful perspective.

A hundred yards from my home is The Evan

Thomas Institute with its charming young mothers, its delightful young staff and its joyous and very ordinary, but extraordinary, babies and tiny kids.

I slip quietly into the back of the room, sit on the floor, lean back against the wall, and I watch the world's most important and most gentle revolution taking place. In five minutes my hopes for the world soar, my spirits skyrocket, my perspective is back in place, and once more it's a great day in the morning.

It's a pleasant room, the Japanese room, with its Japanese *tatami* floor, shoji screens and nothing else except extraordinary people and a vibrant feeling of excitement, love and respect so palpable that everyone who enters there can feel it.

On the opposite side of the room and facing me, three staff members in their late twenties are kneeling. Around them in a semicircle and facing them are twenty mothers in their twenties and thirties. Sitting on the floor in front of the mothers are the very ordinary, quite extraordinary, lovely two- and three-year-old kids. Some of the mothers also have a baby in their arms. No one pays the slightest attention to me or to the other observers, which include a college professor, two schoolteachers, a writer from Britain, an Australian pediatrician and a new mother.

A beautiful little blond two-year-old girl is reading aloud. So absorbed is she in what she is reading that she sometimes giggles as she reads a phrase that touches her sense of humor.

The humor is lost on me because she is reading in Japanese. Although I often work in Japan with Japanese children, my small store of Japanese is not up to her reading. When she reads the phrase that makes her giggle, the other children laugh too. She is reading the Japanese, not in English characters but in the ancient Kanji, the language of Japanese scholars.

There is only one Japanese person in the room. Beautiful, kimono-clad Miki Nakayachi, the Japanese *sensei* interrupts to ask the girl a question. Miki's question and Lindley's answer are both in Japanese, so I understand neither. I remind myself to ask Miki what they were saying that so interested everyone.

Lindley finishes, and Janet Doman, the director of The Institute, asks in English, "Who would like to compose some funny Japanese sentences?"

Several hands shoot up, and Janet chooses Mark, who is three years old. Mark bounces up to take his place beside Suzie Aisen, The Institute's vice director. Suzie places several stacks of large cards before Mark. Each contains a single and, to me, undecipherable Kanji ideograph. Some are nouns or verbs, others articles, adjectives or adverbs.

Mark chooses several cards, lays them out on the floor in an order he chooses and reads them aloud. Everyone laughs, and Janet translates, much to my relief. He has written: "The moose sits on the apple pie."

A two-year-old composes the sentence "The elephant is brushing the strawberry's teeth."

And so in an instant thirty delightful minutes pass.

The staff rises and faces the mothers and children. The children stand up with obvious reluctance, and so do the mothers. Gracefully they all bow to each other. It's such a lovely sight that tears come to my eyes, and I look carefully down at my watch to hide them. I hear laughter because a fifteen-month-old boy has bowed so low that he has lost his balance. He laughs too as he picks himself up.

The reluctance to leave the Japanese language, reading and composing class ends as the cavalcade of mothers and extraordinary but ordinary tiny kids troops down the hall toward the next class, which is advanced math.

I remember how astonishingly far we have come in the fifteen years that have vanished so quickly since May of 1963, when the gentle revolution had begun so quietly with the publication of *How to Teach Your Baby to Read.*

When mothers discovered that they could not only teach their babies to read, but could teach them better and easier at two years of age than the school system was doing at seven, they got the bit firmly in their teeth—and a new and almost indescribably delightful world opened up. A world of mothers and kids. It has within it the potential to change the larger world, in a very short time and almost infinitely for the better.

By 1975 a handful of young, bright and eager mothers had discovered The Evan Thomas Institute and The Evan Thomas Institute had discovered them. Together they taught their babies to read, superbly in English and adequately in two or three other languages. They taught the kids to do math at a rate that left them agog, in shocked but delighted disbelief. They taught their one-, two- and three-year-olds to absorb encyclopedic knowledge of birds, flowers, insects, trees, Presidents, flags, nations, geography and a host of other things. They taught them to do Olympic routines on balance beams, to swim and to play the violin.

In short, they found that they could teach their tiny children absolutely anything they could present to them in an honest and factual way.

Most *interesting* of all, they found that by doing so, they had multiplied their babies' intelligence.

Most *important* of all, they found that doing so was for them and for their babies the most delightful experience they had ever enjoyed together. Their love for each other and, perhaps even more important, their respect for each other multiplied.

The Evan Thomas Institute does not actually teach children at all. It really teaches mothers to teach their children. Here then were these young women, at the prime of life, not at the beginning of the end but rather at the end of the beginning. They were themselves, at twenty-five or at thirty-two, learning to speak Japanese, to read Spanish, to play the violin, to attend concerts, to visit museums, to do gymnastics and a host of other splendid things that most women dream of doing at some dim time in the distant future but that for most people are never realized. That they were doing these things with their own tiny children increased their joy in the doing. Guilt at escaping their children had somehow, and magically, been transformed into pride and a real sense of high purpose for themselves, their children and the contributions they would make to the world.

On a particular morning a year or more ago, when

I had arrived at the math class, Suzie and Janet were presenting math problems to the tiny kids faster than I could assimilate the problems. Their answers were correct—not nearly right but exactly right.

"What," Suzie asked, "is 16 times 19, subtract 151, multiply by 3, add 111, divide by 4 and subtract 51?"

"How far is it from Philadelphia to Chicago?" asked Janet. "And if your car gets 5 miles to the gallon, how many gallons of gas will it take to drive to Chicago?"

"Suppose the car gets 12 miles to the gallon?"

I thought about Giulio Simeone and the day I had asked him what 19 squared was.

"361, but ask me something hard with a big answer."

"Okay," I had responded, searching in my mind for something with a big answer. "How many zeros are there in a sextillion?" Giulio, who was three years old and who likes big numbers, pondered for a few seconds. "21," he announced with a smile. I sat down and wrote out a sextillion. There are 21 zeros in a sextillion.

I had seen such splendid things happen many times before, but they never failed to reastonish me. Nor had it ever failed to restore my soul and my faith that tomorrow would be worth seeing and living.

It had taken us ten years to learn how, but we were finally ready to teach all mothers who wanted to know how to teach their babies to do math. Considering how extraordinarily bright babies are and how easily they learn, it is not surprising that we could teach them. What was incredible was that we had learned how to teach them to do math better than their own parents, who had themselves done the teaching.

How could this be, and how had we learned about it?

2

The Long Road
to Understanding

> Man a dunce uncouth,
> errs in age and youth;
> babies know the truth.
>
> —Swinburne

I was stunned.

Could it possibly be as simple as it seemed to be? If it was, how could I possibly have been so abysmally stupid as to miss it when I had been staring at the answer for so many years? If it was true, I had been a damned fool. I hoped that I had indeed been a damned fool.

It was an odd place to have stumbled on the obvious answer and, at least for me, an even odder time. I was in the Okura Hotel in Tokyo, and it was a little after 6 A.M. I seldom wake so early, since I seldom manage to get to bed much before 2 or 3 A.M.

I had gone to sleep a few hours earlier with the problem very much on my mind.

The team and I were in Tokyo, where we go at least twice a year to teach the parents of Japanese children how to multiply the intelligence of their well babies and their hurt kids. We were quite experienced at this, since we also did it twice a year in Britain, Ireland, Italy, Australia and Brazil, just as we did the same thing full time in America.

The Japanese parents, like the other parents we had been teaching at home in Philadelphia and abroad, were succeeding beautifully.

Virtually all the children could read at far younger ages than did average children; virtually all the children had stored thousands of bits of encyclopedic information in their brains on a myriad of subjects. They also did math at speeds that surpassed that of adults, a fact that was at once marvelous and yet somehow distressing to the adults (although it bothered the children not at all since they didn't know the grown-ups couldn't do it).

The class on How to Teach Your Baby Math had been a review class, since virtually all the two- and three-year-olds were already doing it successfully. The parents, who were delighted that they had successfully taught their kids, were extremely attentive, but were still not clear on my explanation of why kids could do math *faster* and *better* than they themselves could.

I knew the reason that they didn't really understand it was that I didn't really understand, and it was I who was explaining it. Both they and we knew beyond doubt that it *was* so, because the children were doing math beautifully.

Neither the parents nor I had been really satisfied with my answers as to *why*.

Was it purely and simply the very basic and different way we had developed to introduce them to math? If this was the answer, why had we not yet found a single adult who could master the same simple system?

I had gone to bed unhappy with my own complex answers to their questions. I had come awake a few minutes before six, completely alert, which is unusual for me.

Was it conceivable that the answer could be so simple and straightforward? I had considered and rejected a hundred more-complex answers.

Could it possibly be that we adults had so long used symbols to represent facts that (at least in mathematics) we had learned to perceive only the symbols and were not able to perceive the actual facts? It was clear that children could perceive the facts, because they were virtually all doing so.

I recalled the sound advice of Sherlock Holmes, who had proposed that if you eliminate all the factors that are impossible, whatever solution remains must be the answer no matter how improbable it appears to be.

It was the answer.

It's astonishing that we adults have succeeded in keeping the secret of doing math away from children as long as we have. It's a wonder that the tiny kids with all their brightness—and bright they are —didn't catch on. The only reason some careless adult hasn't spilled the beans to the two-year-olds is that we adults haven't known the secret either. But now it's out.

The most important secret is about the kids themselves. We grown-ups have believed that the older you are, the easier it is to learn, and in some things this is true. But it certainly is *not* true concerning languages.

Languages are made up of facts called words, numbers or notes, depending on which language you're talking about. In the learning of pure facts, children can learn *anything* we can present to them in a factual and honest way. What's more, the younger they are, the easier it is.

Words, as everyone knows, are written symbols that represent specific, factual things, actions or thoughts. Musical notes are written symbols that represent specific, factual sounds, and numerals are written symbols that represent specific, factual numbers of objects.

In reading, music and math *most* adults do better than *most* kids, but in distinguishing the *individual* words, notes or numbers all kids learn quicker and much more easily than all adults *if they are given the opportunity young enough*. It is easier for a five-year-old to learn facts than for a six, for a four-year-old than a five, for a three-year-old than a four, for a two-year-old than a three. And by George it is easier for a one-year-old than for a two—if you're willing to be patient enough to wait until he's two to prove it.

It is now abundantly clear that the younger one learns to do something the better he does it. John Stuart Mill could read Greek when he was three. Eugene Ormandy could play the violin when he was three; so could Mozart. Most of the great mathematicians, such as Bertrand Russell, could do arithmetic as small children.

In the learning of mathematics tiny children actually have a staggering *advantage* over adults. In the reading of words we adults can recognize the symbol *or* the fact without effort. Thus either the written word *refrigerator* or the refrigerator itself can be called to mind instantly and easily. Learning the language of music is a little more difficult for adults than for children. If we adults can read music at all, it is much easier to recognize the written note than it is to be sure of the precise sound it represents. Many of us are tone-deaf and are totally unable to identify the actual sound even though we may be capable of reading the symbol. Very few of us have "perfect pitch" and can always identify the exact sound represented by the note. Tiny children can be taught with very little effort to have very close to perfect pitch.

In mathematics the advantage that tiny children have is staggering. We adults recognize the symbols that are called numerals with great ease from the numeral 1 to the numeral 1,000,000 and beyond without effort. We are not, however, able to recognize the actual number of objects beyond ten or so with any degree of reliability.

Tiny children can actually see and almost instantly identify the actual number of objects as *well* as the numeral *if they are given the opportunity to do so early enough in life and before they are introduced to numerals.*

This gives tiny children a staggering advantage over all adults in learning to do and actually to *understand* what is happening in arithmetic.

It will be helpful to the reader's total ultimate understanding if she or he ponders that deceptively simple, but in no way simplistic, fact for a few short chapters. We had pondered that problem for several long years.

Here are some *facts:*

1. Tiny children *want* to learn math.
2. Tiny children *can* learn math (and the younger the child, the easier it is).
3. Tiny children *should* learn math (because it is an advantage to do math better and more easily).

We've devoted a short chapter to each of these vital points.

3

Tiny Children
<u>Want</u> to Learn Math

> Children and genius have the
> same master organ in common
> —inquisitiveness. Let child-
> hood have its way and as it
> began where genius begins, it
> may find what genius finds.
>
> —Edward G. Bulwer-Lytton

While naturally, no child wants to learn math until
he knows that math exists, all children want to absorb information about everything around them,
and under the proper circumstances math is one of
these things.

Here are the Cardinal Points concerning a tiny
child's wanting to learn and his fantastic ability to
learn:

1. The process of learning begins at birth or
   earlier.
2. All babies have a rage to learn.
3. Little kids would rather learn than eat.
4. Kids would much rather learn than play.

5. Tiny kids believe it is their job to grow up.
6. Little kids want to grow up right now.
7. All kids believe learning is a survival skill.
8. They are right in so believing.
9. Tiny children want to learn about *every-thing* and right now.
10. Math is one of the things worth learning about.

There has never been, in the history of man, an adult scientist who has been half so curious as is any child between the ages of four months and four years. We adults have mistaken this superb curiosity about everything as a lack of ability to concentrate.

We have, of course, observed our children carefully, but we have not always understood what their actions mean. For one thing, many people often use two very different words as if they were the same. The words are *learning* and *educating*.

Learning generally refers to the process that goes on in the one who is acquiring knowledge, while *educating* is often the learning process guided by a teacher or school. Although everyone really knows this, these two processes are frequently thought of as one and the same.

Because of this we sometimes feel that since formal education begins at six years of age, the more important processes of learning also begin at six years of age.

Nothing could be further from the truth.

The truth is that a child begins to learn at birth or earlier. By the time he is six years of age and begins his schooling he has already absorbed a fantastic amount of information, fact for fact, perhaps more than he will learn in the rest of his life.

Before a child is six he has learned most of the basic facts about himself and his family. He has learned about his neighbors and his relationships to them, his world and his relationship to it, and a host of other facts that are literally uncountable. Most significantly, he has learned at least one whole language and sometimes more than one. (The chances are very small that he will ever truly master an additional language after he is six.)

All this before he has seen the inside of a classroom.

The process of learning through these early years proceeds at great speed unless we thwart it. If we appreciate and encourage it, the process will take place at a truly unbelievable rate.

A tiny child has, burning within him, a boundless desire to learn.

We can kill this desire entirely only by destroying him completely.

We can come close to quenching it by isolating him. We read occasionally of, say, a thirteen-year-old idiot who is found in an attic chained to a bedpost, presumably because he was an idiot. The reverse is probably the case. It is extremely likely that he is an idiot *because* he was chained to the bedpost. To appreciate this fact we must realize that only psychotic parents would chain any child. A parent chains a child to a bedpost *because* the parent is psychotic, and the result is an idiot child *because* he has been denied virtually all opportunity to learn.

We can *diminish* the child's desire to *learn* by limiting the experiences to which we expose him. Unhappily, we have done this almost universally by drastically underestimating what he can learn.

We can *increase* his learning markedly simply by removing many of the physical restrictions we have placed upon him.

We can *multiply* by many times the knowledge he absorbs if we appreciate his superb capacity for learning and give him unlimited opportunity while simultaneously encouraging him to learn.

Throughout history there have been isolated but numerous cases of people who have actually taught tiny children to learn the most extraordinary things including math, foreign languages, reading, gymnastics and a host of other things by appreciating and encouraging them. In *all* the cases we were able to find, the results of such preplanned home opportunity for children to learn ranged from "excellent" to "astonishing" in producing happy, well-adjusted children with exceptionally high intelligence.

It is very important to bear in mind that these children had *not* been found to have high intelligence first and then been given unusual opportunities to learn, but instead were simply children whose parents decided to expose them to as much information as possible at a very early age.

Once a mother realizes that all tiny children have a rage to learn and have a superb ability to do so, then respect is added to love, and one wonders how she could ever have missed it in the first place.

Look carefully at the eighteen-month-old child and see what he does.

In the first place he drives everybody to distraction.

Why does he? Because he won't stop being curious. He cannot be dissuaded, disciplined or confined out of the desire to learn, no matter how hard we try—and we have certainly tried very hard. He would rather learn than eat or play.

He wants to learn about the lamp and the coffee cup and the electric light socket and the newspaper and everything else in the room—which means that he knocks over the lamp, spills the coffee, puts his finger in the electric light socket and tears up the newspaper. He is learning constantly and, quite naturally, we can't stand it.

From the way he carries on we have concluded that he is hyperactive and unable to pay attention, when the simple truth is that he pays attention to everything. He is superbly alert in every way he can be to learning about the world. He sees, hears, feels, smells and tastes. There is no other way to learn except by these five routes into the brain, and the child uses them all.

He sees the lamp and therefore pulls it down so that he can feel it, hear it, look at it, smell it and taste it. Given the opportunity, he will do all these things to the lamp—and he will do the same to every object in the room. He will not demand to be let out of the room until he has absorbed all he can, through every sense available to him, about every object in the room. He is doing his best to learn, and of course we are doing our best to stop him because his learning process is far too expensive.

We parents have devised several methods of coping with the curiosity of the very young child, and unfortunately, almost all of them are at the expense of the child's learning.

He is aware, if we are not, that learning is for human beings a survival skill. His every instinct tells him so.

Since we are less aware, we have unconsciously devised several methods for the prevention of learning.

The first general method is the give-him-some-thing-to-play-with-that-he-can't-break school of thought. This usually means a nice pink rattle to play with. It may even be a more complicated toy than a rattle, but it's still a toy. Presented with such an object, the child promptly looks at it (which is why toys have bright colors), bangs it to find out if it makes a noise (which is why rattles rattle), feels it (which is why toys don't have sharp edges), tastes it (which is why the paint is nonpoisonous) and even smells it (we have not yet figured out how toys ought to smell, which is why they don't smell at all). This process takes about ninety seconds.

Now that he knows all he wants to know about the toy for the present, the child promptly abandons it and turns his attention to the box in which it came. The child finds the box just as interesting as the toy—which is why we should always buy toys that come in boxes—and learns all about the box. This also takes about ninety seconds. In fact, the child will frequently pay more attention to the box than to the toy itself. Because he is allowed to break the box, he may be able to learn how it is made. This is an advantage he does not have with the toy itself, since we make toys unbreakable, which of course reduces his ability to learn.

The truth of course is that the child never saw the toy as a toy in the first place. He saw both the rattle and the box as being simply new materials from which he had something to learn. The hard and sad truth is that all toys and games are invented by adults to put kids off.

Tiny children never invent either toys or games. They invent tools. Give a child a piece of wood and it immediately becomes a hammer—and he promptly hammers Dad's cherry table. Give a child a clam shell and it instantly becomes a dish.

If you simply watch children you will see dozens of examples of this. Yet, despite all of the evidence that our eyes give us, we too often come to the conclusion that when a child has a short attention span, he just isn't very smart. This deduction insidiously implies that he (like all other children) is not very bright because he is very young. One wonders what our conclusions would be if the two-year-old sat in a corner and quietly played with the rattle for five hours. Probably the parents of such a child would be even more upset—and with good reason.

The second general method of coping with his attempts to learn is the put-him-back-in-the-playpen school of thought.

The only proper thing about the playpen is its name—it is truly a pen. We should at least be honest about such devices and stop saying, "Let's go buy a playpen for the baby." Let's tell the truth and admit that we buy them for ourselves.

Few parents realize what a playpen really costs.

Not only does the playpen restrict the child's ability to learn about the world, which is fairly obvious, but it seriously restricts his neurological growth by limiting his ability to crawl and creep (processes vital to normal growth). This in turn inhibits the development of his vision, manual competence, hand-eye coordination and a host of other things.

We parents have persuaded ourselves that we are buying the playpen to protect the child from hurting himself by chewing on an electric cord or falling down the stairs. Actually, we are penning him up so that *we* do not have to make sure he is safe. In terms of our time, we are being penny-wise and pound-foolish.

The playpen as an implement that prevents learning is unfortunately much more effective than the rattle, because after the child has spent ninety seconds learning about each toy Mother puts in the pen (which is why he will throw each of them out as he finishes learning about it), he is then stuck.

Thus we have succeeded in preventing him from destroying things (one way of learning) by physically confining him. This approach, which puts the child in a physical, emotional and educational vacuum, will not fail so long as we can stand his anguished screams to get out or, assuming that we can stand it, until he's big enough to climb out and renew his search for learning.

Does all the above assume that we are in favor of letting the child break the lamp? Not at all. It assumes only that we have had far too little respect for the small child's desire to learn, despite all the clear indications he gives us that *he wants desper-*

ately to learn everything he can, and as quickly as possible.

We have succeeded in keeping our children carefully isolated from learning in a period of life when the desire to learn is at its peak.

Between birth and four years the ability to absorb information is unparalleled, and the desire to do so is stronger than it will ever be again. Yet during this period we keep the child clean, well fed, safe from the world about him and in a learning vacuum.

It is ironic that when the child is older we will tell him repeatedly how foolish he is for not wanting to learn about astronomy, physics and biology. Learning, we will tell him, is the most important thing in life, and indeed it is.

We have overlooked the other side of the coin.

Learning is the greatest game in life and the most fun. All children are born believing this and will continue to believe this until we convince them that learning is very hard work and unpleasant. Some kids never really learn this lesson and go on through life believing that learning is fun and the only game worth playing. We have a name for such people. We call them geniuses.

We have assumed that children hate to learn essentially because most children have disliked or even despised school. Again we have mistaken schooling for learning. Not all children in school are learning—just as not all children who are learning are doing so in school.

My own experiences in first grade were perhaps typical of what they have been for centuries. In general the teacher told us to sit down, keep quiet, look at her and listen to her while she began a process called teaching, which, she said, would be mutually painful but from which we would learn—or else.

In my own case, that first-grade teacher's prophecy proved to be correct; it was painful, and at least for the first twelve years, I hated every minute of it. I'm sure it was not a unique experience.

In my own case (and I suspect in almost everybody else's) it turned out that the teacher could make me sit down, could make me be quiet, could make me look at her, but could not make me listen and think along with her.

During the rest of that year (and it seemed to me like a hundred years) I found myself in deeper oceans than Cousteau ever visited, on the top of Mount Everest long before Sir Edmund Hillary ever scaled its heights and on the far side of the moon thirty-five years before NASA came into being. I would otherwise have found that century I spent in the first grade a time of crushing boredom interrupted as it was with moments of sheer panic when, during my Jungle Explorations, I dimly heard my teacher calling on "Glenn." It wasn't that I didn't know the answer, it was that I didn't know the question.

I dare dwell on my personal experiences in school only because I believe I was the rule rather than the exception.

Particularly was this so in arithmetic. In first grade we were made to memorize long arithmetic tables such as two times two is four. Being a child, I found this to be dreadfully boring but quite easy. Had I been *two* years old it would have been quite interesting and even easier.

In the second grade it seemed briefly as if things

in arithmetic were looking up. The first day of real multiplication seemed hopeful.

"We're going to multiply 23 by 17," said my teacher. "We put it down this way." Here she wrote on the board:

$$23$$
$$\times\ 17$$

She had me now and I was interested.

"First," she said, "we multiply 7 times 3. What is that, Bobby?"

"21," said Bobby, who had been made to memorize it.

"Yes," said the teacher. "Now we put down the 1 and carry the 2," suiting the action to the words.

"Why do we do that?" I asked with great interest.

"Do what?" my teacher asked, clearly annoyed.

"Why do we put down the 1 and carry the 2?"

"Because it's the *right* thing to do," said the teacher. "Everybody *else* seems to understand it, so we'll go on."

"Now we multiply our 2 by our 7. How much is that, Eleanor?" asked the teacher.

"14," said Eleanor.

The teacher smiled. Not everybody in the class was as stupid as some small boys.

"Now we add the 2 that we borrowed which makes 16, and we put it down here."

"Why do we do that?" I asked.

She turned to me slowly, letting all the class see her endless patience and how it was tried.

"Now, what do you want to know this time, Glenn?"

"Why do we add the 2 that we borrowed to 14 to make 16?" I asked.

"Because," she said with finality, "it is the proper way to do it."

My curiosity was whetted and the fire started. The fire was out of control.

"Why," I persisted, "don't we *subtract* the two we borrowed or why don't we write it down on the *other* side of the 1?"

"Because," said the teacher, "I'm bigger than you are!"

It was the clearest thing anyone ever said to me in all the years in school.

Now of course the conversation I've just described in such detail never actually took place. It *would* have taken place just as I have described it except that I had always known she was bigger than I was. I wasn't very good in arithmetic, but I wasn't stupid enough to miss the fact that my teacher was bigger than I.

She really believed that the *reason* you put down the 1 and carry the 2 was that it was the proper thing to do, the way to do it, and this was enough reason.

I'm sure she believed this because half a century earlier her teacher had told her that the reason you did it that way was that it was the proper way to do it. My teacher had also known that her teacher was bigger than she was.

That this was the *right* way to do it had never seemed to me to be very persuasive or very logical. It still doesn't.

I suppose this is why I've always been apprehensive about mathematics. I'm downright suspicious of all things that are right because somebody (especially somebody bigger than I) *says* they are right. So many such things have turned out *not* to be right.

Learning *is* fun whether teachers think it is or not, and all tiny children know it.

In summary, babies want to learn about everything, they want to learn about it right now and, having no judgment at all, they want to learn about everything with a fine impartiality.

Part of that *everything* is mathematics, and mathematics is worth learning about.

Strangely, mathematics, which is so difficult for adults to learn, is easier for a one-year-old to learn than anything else.

4

Tiny Children
<u>Can</u> Learn Math

*(and the younger the child,
the easier it is)*

Feel the dignity of a child. Do
not feel superior to him, for you
are not.

—Robert Henri

Virtually everybody loves little kids, but very few
adults can honestly be said to respect them. This is
because we believe that in every way we are superior to kids. We are taller, heavier, smarter. And, we
might well add, a good deal more arrogant.

It is true that we are taller than a little child and
heavier, but when it comes to smarter, we should
be careful about rushing to a conclusion.

ALL BABIES ARE LINGUISTIC GENIUSES

Linguistic ability is a built-in function of the
human brain.

Let's consider the absolutely extraordinary ability that all babies have to learn a language, a miracle beyond measure that we all take totally for granted. Understanding and speaking a language is complex beyond belief and is the single factor that most clearly separates us human beings from the other creatures of the earth.

There are 450,000 words in the English language, and there are 100,000 words in a first-rate vocabulary. Those words can be put together in a virtually limitless number of combinations.

Yet in a normal conversation we encode a message as fast as we can speak. We think in thoughts, and when we speak we often have no idea of how the sentence, paragraph or conversation will end. In short, we encode a message into words, sentences and paragraphs as fast as we can talk. This miracle is not the end. As fast as we can talk by encoding our thoughts into words, that same message is being decoded from words, sentences or paragraphs back into thoughts by the listener.

It is not surprising that we sometimes misunderstand each other; it is breathtaking that we most frequently do understand each other.

Only the human brain is capable of this incredible feat. No computer in existence, nor all the computers in existence hooked together, could carry on a human conversation or even approximate one.

Yet we take it all totally for granted. So complex is human language that only a small proportion of adults ever learn a second language and a very, very small percentage ever learn a foreign tongue perfectly.

ALL BABIES LEARN A FOREIGN LANGUAGE PRIOR TO TWO YEARS OF AGE

This miracle of speech is a built-in function of the human brain.

Any adult foolish enough to get himself into a language-learning contest with *any* average infant would be a fool indeed and would learn that adults are *not* brighter than babies when it comes to the dreadfully complicated business of learning a foreign language.

It must be remembered that all babies learn a foreign language prior to two years of age, speak it fluently by four years of age and speak it perfectly (to their own environment) by six years of age.

We must bear in mind that to a baby born today in Philadelphia, English is a completely foreign language. It is to him no more or no less foreign than French, German, Swahili, Japanese or Portuguese.

And who teaches this baby to perform the miracle of learning this foreign language called English? In our adult arrogance we believe that we do, when, in truth, we actually teach him *Mommy, Daddy* and a few dozen other words. He teaches himself the other tens of thousands of words he will learn, by merely listening to us talk. He does so with the use of his superb human cortex. Only we human beings have such a cortex; only we human beings talk in a contrived, symbolic language, and that unique human speech is a product of the unique human cortex. The human brain gives us the capacity for *language*, and we humans have invented *lan-guages*, hundreds of them.

It is equally true, as everyone knows, that if a child is born into a bilingual household he will speak two languages. If he is born into a trilingual household he will speak three languages—and with no more effort than he spent in learning one, which is no effort at all.

So casually do we accept this unbelievable feat that we give it little or no thought—unless, of course, he does not speak. If, because of brain injury, a child does not speak, then his parents are willing to bring him as far as twelve thousand miles to The Institutes in Philadelphia. Thousands do. Then, and only then, does the size of the miracle become obvious.

Let's compare the performances of an average baby with an adult trying to learn a foreign tongue or even with an adolescent.

Again my own experience may be typical. As a child I wanted very much to learn French. Since in those days every one believed (against all the evidence) that the older you were the easier it was to learn a language, the result was that French was not taught until high school. I was eager to learn, and the fact is that I established some sort of record in my high school. I flunked four consecutive years of French. My record was not in flunking—lots of students flunked. My record was in obstinacy. I was the only one who kept trying for four years. *Nobody* in my class came close to learning to speak French.

I can still remember my teacher, with his fingers on the bridge of his nose and his eyes closed, saying to me, "Mr. Doman, that's one of those awful sen-

tences like 'I seen him when he done it.' " I'm sure
that my French teacher has long since gone to his
reward, and I'm equally sure that his reward is not
having to teach young adults French. Mr. Zimmer-
man can rest easily in his grave because I no longer
say, "I seen him when he done it" in French. Now,
forty years and a dozen trips to France later, I can't
really say much of anything in French, and it isn't
because I don't try.

I was simply too old, in my teens. Yet every average French six-year-old speaks French perfectly
to his own environment. If his family members say
the French equivalent of "I seen him when he done
it," then of course so does he. If his dad is the head
of the French Department at the Sorbonne, then
our six-year-old speaks classical French with fine
grammar and he has not yet seen a teacher or heard
the word *grammar*.

What does all this mean, and what does it have to
do with a tiny child's ability to learn math?

Everything.

IT IS EASIER TO TEACH A ONE-YEAR-OLD
A FOREIGN LANGUAGE
THAN IT IS TO TEACH A SEVEN-YEAR-OLD

Linguistic ability is a built-in function of his
human brain.

As we have just seen.

IT IS EASIER TO TEACH A ONE-YEAR-OLD
TO READ A LANGUAGE
THAN IT IS TO TEACH A SEVEN-YEAR-OLD

This too is a built-in function of his human brain.
Tens of thousands of mothers have taught one-,

two- and three-year-olds to read and read well, while 30 percent of children in all school systems fail to read at all or fail to read at grade level. The Philadelphia school system produces many eighteen-year-old high school graduates who cannot read labels on jars. (This deplorable situation is not confined to Philadelphia.)

They have simply been taught too late.

IT IS EASIER TO TEACH A ONE-YEAR-OLD MATH
THAN IT IS TO TEACH A SEVEN-YEAR-OLD

Mathematical ability is a built-in function of his human brain.

English, French, Italian and all other languages contain tens of thousands of basic symbols called words which are combined in endless intricate relationships of phrases, sentences and paragraphs called grammar, which all well human beings master as babies and children.

Math contains ten basic symbols called 1, 2, 3, 4, 5, 6, 7, 8, 9 and 0.

The astounding question is not why babies and tiny kids can do math faster and more easily than adults, but rather why adults who can deal in a spoken language with ease cannot do math faster and more easily than they can talk.

YOU CAN TEACH A BABY ANYTHING
THAT YOU CAN PRESENT TO HIM
IN AN HONEST AND FACTUAL WAY

It is a built-in function of his human brain.

Babies can be taught facts with the speed of summer lightning, which is in itself a fact that staggers the adult imagination. Most especially is this true if the facts are presented in a precise, discrete and nonambiguous way.

Words, musical notes and numbers are particularly precise, discrete and nonambiguous. This is true whether they are written or sounded. The written word *nose* always means nose, and the spoken sound always means nose. The written musical note middle C always means middle C, and so also does the sound of middle C. The written word *six* always means six, and so does the sound six.

These are facts, and kids learn them a mile a minute. The younger they are, the faster they learn them.

The problem is that we adults divide information into two kinds, the kind we call concrete and the kind we call abstract. Concrete things are those we understand easily; abstract things are those we understand less well.

Then, being adults, we very often insist on teaching children abstractions, which are those things we understand least, while depending on children to learn the precise, discrete, nonambiguous facts by themselves.

In short, we insist on giving tiny kids our opinions rather than the facts. In short, we insist on programming into our kids our own opinions, which very often prove to be wrong. We shall see how serious a mistake this is.

That all tiny kids learn thousands of spoken words before they are three and that thousands of kids can read them as well proves that you can teach a baby anything that you can present to him in an honest and factual way. This includes that very factual and much simpler language called math.

THE ABILITY TO TAKE IN RAW FACTS
IS AN INVERSE FUNCTION OF AGE

It is a built-in function of his human brain.

Myths die slowly indeed, even in the face of overwhelming evidence to the contrary. No myth dies more slowly than the belief that the older you are, the easier it is to learn. The truth is exactly the reverse. The older we are, the more wisdom we acquire, but the younger we are, the easier it is to take in facts and the easier they are to store.

It must by now be obvious to the reader, as it is to all those who know the staff of The Institutes, that we have for all babies' ability to learn and all parents' ability to teach, a respect that borders on reverence. Yet I have never seen a two-year-old wise enough not to fall out of a tenth-story window or to drown himself, given opportunity to do so.

Wisdom, the tiny child does not have; but the ability to take in raw facts—in prodigious amounts —he does have, and the *younger* he is, right down to the early months of life, the *easier* this is.

IT IS EASIER TO TEACH A ONE-YEAR-OLD
ANY SET OF FACTS
THAN IT IS TO TEACH A SEVEN-YEAR-OLD

It is a built-in function of his human brain.

When we speak of a "set of facts" we mean a group of *related* facts. Thus a group of portraits of Presidents of the United States would be a set of facts. Cards each containing the flag of a different nation would be a set of facts, cards each containing a different number of like objects would be a set of facts, and so on.

There are huge advantages in presenting facts to a tiny child in sets; this is discussed in great detail in the forthcoming book *How to Multiply Your Baby's Intelligence.*

That a one-year-old learns sets of facts more quickly than a seven-year-old (and that a seven-year-old learns them more quickly than a thirty-year-old) has been demonstrated thousands of times at The Institutes. Mothers teaching such sets of facts at home find that their children learn them—and retain them longest—in reverse order of age, and that the mother herself learns them the most slowly of all—and forgets them the most quickly. We have also found this to be true with the staff itself, to their mixed chagrin and delight.

With all of the sets of facts presented to the tiny children this fact is the most clear when teaching mathematics.

IF YOU TEACH A TINY CHILD THE FACTS HE WILL INTUIT THE RULES

It is a built-in function of the human brain.

Of all of the unusual things this book has to say, it is possible that this quiet point is the most important. To state it in a slightly different way, if you teach him the *facts* of a body of knowledge he will discover the laws by which it operates. A beautiful example of this exists in the mistakes that tiny children make in grammar. This apparent paradox was pointed out by the brilliant Russian author Kornei Chukovski in his book *From Two to Five* (University of California Press).

A three-year-old looks out a window and says, "Here comes the mailer."

"Who?" we ask.

"The mailer."

We look out the window and see the mailman. We chuckle at the childish mistake and tell the child that he is not called the mailer but the mailman.

We then dismiss the matter. Suppose that instead we asked ourselves the question "Where did the child get the word *mailer?*" Surely no adult taught him the word *mailer*. Then where did he get it? I've been thinking about it for fifteen years, and I am convinced that there is only one possibility. The three-year-old must have reviewed the language to come to the conclusion that there are certain verbs (a word he's never heard) such as *run, hug, kiss, sail* and *paint* and that if you put the sound *er* on the end of them they become nouns (another word he's never heard) and you have *runner, hugger, kisser, sailor, painter,* and so on. That's a whale of an accomplishment. When did you, the reader, last review a language to discover a law? May I suggest when you were three? Still we say, it is a mistake because he is not the mailer, he is the mailman, and so the child is wrong. Wrong word, yes, but right law. The child was quite correct about the law of grammar he had discovered. The problem is that English is irregular and thus, to a degree, a problem. If it were regular the three-year-old would have been right.

The tiny child has a huge ability to discover the laws if we teach him the facts.

It is not possible to discover the facts (concrete) if we are taught only the rules (abstractions).

Let's look at this as it applies to math.

IF YOU TEACH A TINY CHILD
THE FACTS ABOUT MATH
HE WILL DISCOVER THE RULES

This is *not* a built-in function of the human brain, since we human beings have invented mathematics and in some ways taught it imperfectly. Not all human beings have invented math as all human beings *have* invented languages. We have lived among several tribes, such as some in the Xingu territory of Brazil, who do not count at all. Others count only to five.

If you teach a child the facts of mathematics, and the facts upon which mathematics is based are numbers—such as one, two, three, four, five, six—rather than numerals—1, 2, 3, 4, 5, 6, or I, II, III, IV, V, VI —he will discover the rules of mathematics which we call addition, subtraction, multiplication, division, algebra and so on. We shall see precisely how he can do this in the chapter on "How to Teach Your Baby Math."

NOTE: In the following pages the word *number* means the actual quantity or true value, while the word *numeral* means the symbol we use to represent the actual quantity.

We human beings are so very much interested in theories and reasons that we tend to obscure reality. Some portions of this book may be a good example of my own need to understand reasons and to explain them.

To prevent our students and ourselves from losing sight of reality, we use a sign containing the following initials—W. K. I. I. S. B. W. D. I.—and all students are required to write them down on the first day of class.

The following dialogue is extremely common between the staff and parents, professionals and students.

> STUDENT: But how do you *know* you can teach tiny babies math (reading, speaking Japanese, playing the violin, etc.)?
>
> INSTRUCTOR: How did the Wright brothers *know* they could fly?
>
> STUDENT: Well, in the end, I suppose, because they did it.
>
> INSTRUCTOR: That's how we know.

W. K. I. I. S. B. W. D. I. means:
We know it is so because we do it.
Tiny children *are* doing math better and more easily than adults. Hundreds of tiny children are presently doing math and doing it with true understanding of what is happening. Only a minute percentage of adults truly understand what actually happens in math.

5

Tiny Children
Should Learn Math

*(because it is an advantage
to do math more easily and better)*

> Mathematics possesses not
> only truth but supreme beauty.
>
> —Bertrand Russell

There are two vitally important reasons why tiny children *should* do math. The first reason is the obvious and less important reason: Doing math is one of the highest functions of the human brain—of all creatures on earth, only people can do math.

Doing math is one of the most important functions of life, since daily it is vital to civilized human living. From childhood to old age we are concerned with math. The child in school is faced with mathematical problems every day, as are the housewife, the carpenter, the businessman and the space scientist.

The second reason is even more important. Children should learn to do math at the youngest possible age because of the effect it will have on the physical growth of the brain itself and the product of that physical growth—what we call intelligence.

We have spent thirty-five years searching for understanding of how the human brain grows. There are five points of vital importance which all have to do with how the brain grows.

FUNCTION DETERMINES STRUCTURE

This is an ancient and well-known law of architecture, engineering, medicine and human growth. In human terms this law means that I am what I am because of what I do.

Lumberjacks are hard and muscular because they chop down trees all day. People who lead lives that permit no exercise are soft and not muscular. It is obvious that the biceps grow by use. Weight lifters are a clear illustration of this. If I lift a 25-pound weight daily my biceps will grow. If you lift a 50-pound weight daily your biceps will grow even more. You will then have two advantages over me. You will be able to lift twice as much as I, and secondly, if we are both going to lift 25 additional pounds I will have to double my ability but you will have to increase yours only 50 percent. Concerning the muscles, this is well known and understood. What is not well known and not understood is that this is also true of the brain.

THE BRAIN, LIKE THE BICEPS, GROWS BY USE

The entire back half of the brain is made up of incoming sensory pathways. All these incoming pathways can be divided among the five senses. Everything Albert Einstein or Leonardo da Vinci ever learned in life, everything you or tiny children have ever learned in life entered the brain through these five pathways through which we hear, feel, see, taste and smell.

These five pathways actually grow by use. This is to say that the more messages that pass over the visual pathway, the auditory pathway, the tactile pathway, the gustatory pathway and the olfactory pathway, the larger these pathways will grow and the more easily they will operate. The fewer messages that pass over them, the more slowly they will grow and the less efficiently they will operate. If virtually no messages pass over them, there will be virtually no growth.

We have already mentioned the thirteen-year-old idiot who is found chained to a bedpost in an attic and who is an idiot precisely *because* he has been chained to a bedpost.

When a well baby is born he is born with all these pathways (which we must remember constitute half the brain) intact but immature. It is precisely the light, sound, feeling, smell, and taste impulses passing over these pathways which cause them to grow, mature and become increasingly efficient. Which is exactly why children should read, do math, learn a dozen languages, know great art and exercise as many other sensory skills as possible at the earliest possible ages. Reading, as an example, actually grows the visual pathways. Listening to great music grows the auditory pathways—which incidentally is why parents should talk endlessly to their children. Which brings us to the question of *content*.

The content of the message should be of the highest order. Good language goes into the baby's brain as easily as baby talk, Beethoven goes in as easily as "Pop Goes the Weasel," great art goes in as easily as "Kiddy Cartoons." The possibilities are endless.

The idea of "Reading Readiness" (and all the other "Readinesses") is sheer nonsense. To say that a child is ready to read at five or six is not only nonsense, it is downright dangerous to children. Readiness is *created* in children, and if it isn't created, as it usually is by accident, or as it rarely is, on purpose, it won't come about at all. Witness the child chained to the bedpost.

That the brain grows by use has been known to the neurophysiologists for more than half a century. There have been animal experiments by the hundreds which prove this to be so beyond question. Outstanding among the great scientists in this field have been such geniuses as the Russian Boris Klosovskii and the American David Krech.

For many years Krech and his associates at Berkeley divided newborn rats into two identical groups. One group was raised in an environment of sensory deprivation with little to see, feel, hear, taste or smell. The other group was raised in an environment of sensory enrichment with a great deal to see, feel, hear, taste and smell. He would then test the intelligence of the rats in normal life situations and later sacrifice the rats and measure, weigh and examine their brains microscopically.

Krech's conclusions were that rats that were raised in sensory deprivation had small, undeveloped, stupid brains, while rats that were raised amid sensory enrichment had large, highly developed, highly intelligent brains. Such experiments with such conclusions are myriad.

The front half of the brain is composed of the motor pathways by which we respond to incoming information. They also grow by use. Which is why physical "readiness" as a function of age is also nonsense. Tiny kids can and should swim, do Olympic gymnastics, dance and pursue all other worthwhile physical activities at one and two years of age. They should because they can and because both the body and the brain grow by physical use —as does intelligence.

THE BRAIN IS THE ONLY CONTAINER THAT HAS THIS CHARACTERISTIC: THE MORE YOU PUT INTO IT THE MORE IT WILL HOLD

We have just seen that the brain grows by use and that the more you use it, the better it will function.

But is there some limit to the brain's growth?

For all practical purposes the answer to this question would appear to be that the most advanced human brain more than ten thousand million (which in the United States is called ten billion) neurons that are fully capable of functioning. *Each* of these neurons has hundreds or even thousands of interconnections with other neurons. The number of combinations and permutations this makes possible simply boggles the mind of all save some theoretical mathematicians. For human purposes the possibilities can be safely said to be virtually endless.

It is safe to say that the brain could hold more than we could put into it in many lifetimes—but the more you put into it the better it works.

Math is one of the most useful things you can put into the tiny child's brain.

IF YOU IMPROVE ONE FUNCTION OF THE BRAIN
YOU IMPROVE ALL FUNCTIONS TO SOME DEGREE

There are six functions of the brain which are unique to man. Each of these is a function of the unique human cortex. The first three of these functions are motor in nature:

1. MOBILITY: Only human beings can stand erect on two legs and walk in perfect cross-pattern swinging opposite arms and legs in unison.
2. LANGUAGE: Only humans speak in a contrived, symbolic language that conveys ideas and feelings.
3. MANUAL COMPETENCE: Only human beings can oppose thumb to forefinger and write that symbolic language that we have invented.

These unique motor skills are based on three unique sensory skills:

4. VISION: Only humans can see in such a way as to read that symbolic written language we humans have invented.

5. AUDITORY: Only human beings can hear in such a way as to understand that symbolic spoken language we have invented.
6. TACTILE: Only human beings can feel a complex object and identify it by touch alone.

So vastly interconnected are each of these brain functions that if one could imagine these six functions as each being a cannonball each attached to the other by an iron chain, one could see that it would be impossible to raise one of them very high without pulling the others up to some small or large degree. The child who knows the language of reading finds it easier to learn the language of math.

Conversely, it is not possible to hold one of these functions down without to some degree holding down the others.

The blind child does not run as well as the sighted child.

INTELLIGENCE IS A RESULT OF THINKING

The world has looked at this point exactly in reverse. We have believed thinking to be a result of intelligence. Surely it is true that without intelligence we could not think. But which came first, the chicken or the egg?

We humans are born with the glorious gift of the genes of Homo sapiens. They are the genes of Leonardo, Shakespeare, Einstein, Mozart, Pauling, Russell, Dart, Jefferson and a host of others. But the human brain is not a gift until it is used. We are born with the *potential* brain of all the human greats (and all the scoundrels); intelligence is a result of what we do with it. Intelligence is a result of thinking.

Math is one important way of putting huge stores of information into the brain and is an important way of thinking.

6

How Is It Possible
For Infants to Do
Instant Math?

The question is not "How is it possible for infants to do instant math?" but rather, "How is it possible for adults who speak a language *not* to do instant math?"

The problem is that in math we have mixed up the symbol, 5, with the fact,

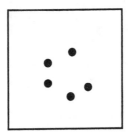

When the problem is on the order of 5 or

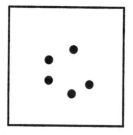

it is no problem since the adult can perceive the symbol or the fact successfully from one

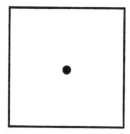

up to about 12

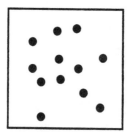

with some degree of reliability.

From 12

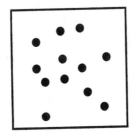

to about 20

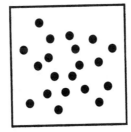

the reliability of even the most perceptive adult
tends to descend sharply.
From 20

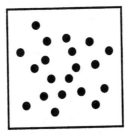

upward one is guessing and almost invariably guessing very badly indeed.

Children who already know symbols, for example 5, 7, 10, 13, but who do not know the facts

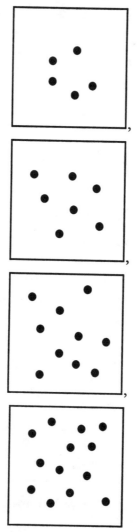

are completely unable to do instant math.

Tiny children, however, see things precisely as they *are* while we adults tend to see things as we believe them to be or as we believe that they should be.

I find it maddening that while I completely understand how children of two years can do instant math I am unable to do the same. The reason I fail to do instant math is that if you say "seventy-nine" to me I am able to see only:

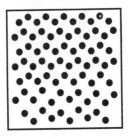

I am not able to see:

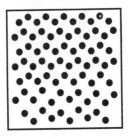

It is not precisely true to say that I cannot "see" the above. I can "see" it but I cannot "perceive" it.

Tiny children can.

In order for tiny children to perceive the truth of one (1) which is actually:

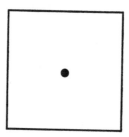

we need only show the child the fact:

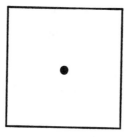

and say, "This is called one."
We next present him with the fact:

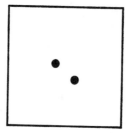

and say, "This is two."

Next we say, "This is three," showing the child:

and so on. We need to present each of these a very small number of times until the infant is able to perceive and retain the truth.

The adult mind, when faced with the fact, is inclined to astonishment, and many adults would rather believe that a child who is able to recognize:

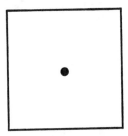

to

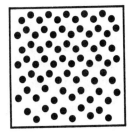

is in some way psychic than believe that a two-year-old can perform a task which we consider to be intellectual in nature and which we grown-ups cannot perform.

The next straw at which we grasp is the belief that the child is not truly recognizing the number but rather the pattern in which the numbers occur.

Any one-year-old worth his salt who has not been sucked into recognizing symbols before he recognizes the facts, can tell you at a cursory glance that:

or whatever other way you choose to arrange the facts are all what we call—27. Sorry, we fooled you—in fact it's forty, not 27!

What we grown-ups can only see if you present us with the symbol "40".

The kids are not fooled regardless of the form in which you present it and see only the truth, while we adults will actually have to count it up if you present it in any random pattern or to multiply it if you present it in an orderly columnar way. Thus if we present the fact in this form:

●●

we solve the problem by actually counting while the tiny child sees the truth at a glance.

If we present the truth in columnar form:

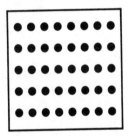

adults are inclined to count the number of rows across which we see as 8 and the number down which we see as 5 and then to use a mathematical recipe which we see as:

$$\begin{array}{r} 8 \\ \times\ 5 \\ \hline 40 \end{array}$$

or as $8 \times 5 = 40.$

This incredibly slow process has almost nothing to recommend it except that it ultimately comes to a correct conclusion. However, even when it comes to the correct conclusion, which we see as 40, we have no idea what 40 actually means except by comparison with something else, such as the number of dollars I earn in a day, or a month plus ten days. The child sees the absolute truth which is that :

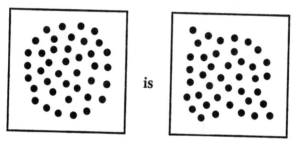

is

No more or less.

If we must have the comparison with a month then it is fair to say that any child who has been given the chance to see the truth knows that September, April, June and November have:

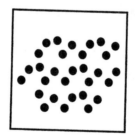

And that if you must compare what we call 40 with a month then what we are talking about is:

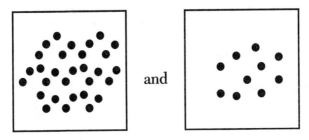 and

as any child can plainly see.

7

How to Teach
Your Baby

We mothers are the potters and
our children the clay.

—Winifred Sackville Stoner
Natural Education

Most sets of instructions begin by saying that unless
they are followed precisely, they won't work.

In contrast to that, it is almost safe to say that no
matter how poorly you expose your baby to mathematics, he is almost sure to learn more than he
would if you hadn't done it; so this is one game
which you will win to some degree no matter how
badly you play it. You would have to do it incredibly
badly to produce no result.

Nonetheless, the more cleverly you play the game
of teaching your tiny child to do math, the quicker
and the better your child will learn.

There are some things to remember.

Bear in mind that when we use the word *numeral*

we mean the symbols that represent the quantity or true value, such as 1, 5, or 9. When we use the word *number* we mean the actual quantity of objects themselves, such as one, five, or nine:

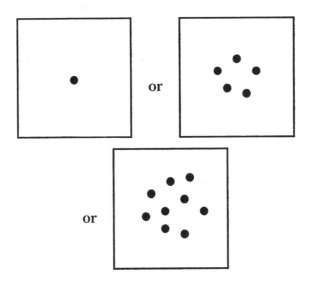

It is in this difference between true value or quantity and its symbolic representation by the use of symbols to represent actual quantity that tiny children find their advantage over adults.

You can teach your baby to do mathematics even if you aren't very good at doing it yourself. This chapter tells you how. It will be even easier if you have already taught him to read.

If you play correctly the game of learning mathematics both you and your child will enjoy it immensely. It takes less than a half-hour a day.

Here are eight additional points to remember about the child himself before discussing how to teach him.

1. Before the age of five a child can easily absorb tremendous amounts of information. If the child is younger than four it will be easier and more effective, before three even easier and much more effective, and before two the easiest and most effective of all.
2. The child before five can accept information at a remarkable rate.
3. The more information a child absorbs before the age of five, the more he retains.
4. The child before five has a tremendous amount of energy.
5. The child before five has a monumental desire to learn.
6. The child before five can learn to read and wants to learn to read.
7. All tiny children are linguistic geniuses.
8. The child before five learns an entire language and can learn as many languages as are presented to him.

Mathematics *is* a language and he can learn to speak it and read it as readily as any other language.

TEACHING BASICS

At What Age to Begin

Beyond two years of age, recognizing quantity or true value gets harder every year.

One year of age or younger is the ideal time to begin if you want to expend the least amount of time and energy in teaching your child mathematics.

You can really begin the process of teaching your baby right from birth. After all, we speak to the baby at birth—this helps the auditory pathway to grow. We can also provide the language of mathematics through the eye—this helps the visual pathway to grow. This process is discussed in Chapter 12.

There are two *vital* points involved in teaching your child:

1. Your attitude and approach.
2. The size and orderliness of the teaching materials.

Parent Attitude and Approach

In all history there has never been a more incorrect assumption than that children do not want to learn. Children want desperately to learn and to learn about everything.

Children begin to learn at or before birth and they learn intuitively. At birth the thought processes are instinctive and inevitable. In all children of *any* age thinking and learning are inevitable. The one year old child believes that learning is necessary, inescapable and the greatest adventure in his life.

Learning *is* the greatest adventure of life. Learning *is* desirable, vital, unavoidable and, above all, life's greatest and most stimulating game. The child believes this and will always believe this—unless we persuade him that it isn't true.

The cardinal rule is that both parent and child must joyously approach learning mathematics as the superb game that it is.

Those educators and psychologists who say that we must not teach tiny children lest we steal their precious childhood by inflicting learning upon them tell us nothing about a child's attitude toward learning—but they certainly tell us a great deal about what they themselves feel about learning.

The parent must never forget that learning is life's most exciting game—it is *not* work.

Learning is a reward; it is not a punishment.

Learning is a pleasure; it is not a chore.

Learning is a privilege; it is not denial.

The parent must always remember this and must never do anything to destroy this natural attitude in the child.

There is a fail-safe law you must never forget. It is this: If you aren't having a wonderful time and your child isn't having a wonderful time—stop. You are doing something wrong.

The Best Time to Teach

Mother must never play this game unless she *and* her child are happy and in good form. If a child is irritable, tired or hungry it is not a good time to do the math program. Find out what is bothering him and handle it.

If mother is cranky or out of sorts, this is not a good time to do the math program. On a bad day it is best not to play the math game at all. Every mother and child experience days when they are at odds or things just don't seem to be going smoothly. It is a wise mother who puts away her math program on such days, recognizing full well that there are many more happy days than cranky ones and that the joy of learning math will be enhanced by choosing the very best and happiest moments to pursue it.

The Best Duration

Make sure that the length of time you play the game is very short. At first it will be played three times a day, but each session will involve only a few seconds.

In regard to determining when to end each session of learning, the parent should exercise great foresight.

Always stop before your child wants to stop.

The parent must know what the child is thinking a little bit before the child knows it and must stop.

If the parent always observes this fact, the child will beg the parent to play the math game and the parent will be nurturing rather than destroying the child's natural desire to learn.

The Manner of Teaching

Whether a math session consists of the opportunity to learn to recognize quantity or learn addition or subtraction, your enthusiasm is the key. Children love to learn and they do it *very quickly.* Therefore you must show your material *very quickly.* We adults do almost everything too slowly for children and there is no area where this is more painfully demonstrated than the way adults teach little children. Generally we expect a child to sit and stare at his materials, to look as if he is concentrating on them. We expect him to look a bit unhappy in order to demonstrate that he is really learning. But children don't think learning is painful, grown-ups do.

When you show your cards do so as fast as you can. You will become more and more expert at this as you do it. Practice a bit on father until you feel comfortable. The materials are carefully designed to be large and clear so that you can show them very quickly and your child will see them easily.

Sometimes when a mother speeds up she is apt to become a bit mechanical and lose the natural enthusiasm and "music" in her voice. It *is* possible to maintain enthusiasm *and* good meaningful sound *and* go very quickly all simultaneously. It is important that you do. Your child's interest and enthusiasm for his math sessions will be closely related to three things:

1. The speed at which materials are shown.
2. The amount of new material.
3. The joyous manner of mother.

The more speed, the more new material and the more joy—the better.

This point of speed, all by itself, can make the difference between a successful session and one that is too slow for your very eager, bright child.

Children don't stare—they don't *need* to stare—they absorb and they do so instantly, like sponges.

Introducing New Material

It is wise at this point to talk about the rate at which each individual child should learn mathematics or, for that matter, learn anything.

Don't be afraid to follow your child's lead. You may be astonished at the size of his hunger and at the rate at which he learns.

We adults were raised in a world that taught us that one must memorize "2 + 2 = 4." We drilled such problems over and over. We often did the same ten or twenty equations again and again. For most of us this endless drilling on a very narrow body of information was the beginning of the end of our attention and interest in the subject of arithmetic.

Instead of twenty addition equations drilled over and over how about one thousand done quickly and joyously? You don't need to be a mathematical genius to know that one thousand addition equations are a great deal more than twenty. But the real point here is not merely the fact that children can hold much more information than we offer them. The important point is what happens when you show the twenty-first addition equation or the one thousand and first equation. This is where the secret of teaching very young children lies.

In the former case the effect of the introduction of the twenty-first equation (when a child has seen the first twenty *ad infinitum* and *ad nauseum*) will be to send him running in the opposite direction as fast as possible. This is the basic principle that is followed in formal education. We adults are experts on how deadly this approach can be. We lived through twelve years of it.

In the latter case the one thousand and first equation is eagerly awaited. The joy of discovery and learning something new is honored and the natural curiosity and love of learning which is born in every child is fed as it should be.

Unfortunately, one method closes the door on learning, sometimes forever. Fortunately, the other opens the door wide and secures it against future attempts to close it.

It is essential to your child's intellectual health and happiness that you offer him a wide selection of mathematical food for thought.

Consistency

It is wise to organize yourself and your materials before you begin because once you begin you will want to establish a consistent program. A modest program done consistently and happily will be infinitely more successful than an over-ambitious program that overwhelms mother and therefore occurs very sporadically. An on-again-off-again program will not be effective. Seeing the materials repeatedly but quickly is vital to mastering them. Your child's enjoyment is derived from real knowledge and this can best be accomplished with a program done daily.

However, sometimes it *is* necessary to put the program away for a few days. This is no problem as long as it does not occur too often. Occasionally it may be vital to put it away for several weeks or even months. For example, a new baby's arrival, moving, traveling, or an illness in the family cause major disruptions to any daily routine. During such upheavals it is best to put your program away *completely*. Use this time to talk to your child about mathematics in everyday life, which requires nothing more than pointing out how many fingers are on one hand or how many flowers there are in the vase or how many stairs there are from the second floor down to the first floor.

Do not try to do a halfway program during these times. It will be frustrating for you and your child. When you are ready to go back to a consistent program start back exactly where you left off. Do not go back and start over again.

Whether you decide to do a modest math program or an extensive program, do whatever suits you *consistently.* You will see your child's enjoyment and confidence grow daily.

Testing

Teaching is giving your child new information as you would give him a gift—testing is asking for it back.

Teaching is a natural and joyous process—testing is unpleasant at best and hateful at worst.

Teach your child, do not test him.

We will discuss testing versus problem-solving in Chapter 10.

Material Preparation

The materials used in teaching your child mathematics are extremely simple. They are based on many years of work on the part of a very large team of child brain develop-mentalists who studied how the human brain grows and functions. They are designed in complete recognition of the fact that mathematics is a *brain* function. They recognize the virtues and limitations of the tiny child's visual apparatus and are designed to meet all of his needs from visual crudeness to visual sophistication and from brain function to brain learning.

All math cards should be made on fairly stiff white posterboard so that they will stand up under the not-always-gentle handling they will receive.

In order to begin you will need:

1. A good supply of white posterboard cut into 11" by 11" square cards. If possible, purchase these already cut to the size you want. This will save you a lot of cutting which is much more time consuming than the remainder of the material preparation.You will need at least one hundred of these to make your initial set of materials.

2. You will also need 5,050 self adhesive red dots, 3/4" in diameter, to make cards 1-100. The Dennison Company makes PRES-a-ply labeling dots which are perfect for this purpose.

3. A large, red, felt-tipped marker. Get the widest tip available—the fatter the marker the better.

You will notice that the materials begin with large red dots. They are red simply because red is attractive to the small child. They are so designed in order that the baby's visual pathway, which is initially immature, can distinguish them readily and without effort. Indeed, the very act of seeing them will in itself speed the development of his visual pathway so that when we eventually teach numerals he will be able to see these numerals and learn them more easily than he otherwise would have.

You will begin by making the cards that you will use to teach your child quantity or the true value of numbers. To do this you will make a set of cards containing the red dots, from a card with one red dot to a card with one hundred red dots. This is time consuming but it is not difficult. There are, however, a few helpful hints that will make your life easier when you are making these materials:

1. Start with the one hundred card and work *backwards* down to one. The higher numbers are harder and you will be more careful at the start than at the finish.
2. Count out the precise number of dots *before* applying them to the card. (You'll have trouble in counting them after you have put them on the card especially when doing cards above twenty).
3. Write the numeral in pencil or pen on all four corners of the back of the card *before* you place the correct number of dots on the front of the card.
4. Be sure *not* to place dots in a pattern such as a square, circle, triangle or diamond or a shape of any other sort.
5. Place dots on the cards in a totally random way working outward from the middle making certain that they do not overlap or touch each other.

6. Be careful to leave a little margin around the
   edges of your cards. This will provide a little
   space for your fingers to curl around the card
   and insure that you are not covering a dot with
   your fingers when you show the cards.

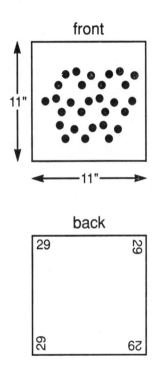

Making the above materials does take some time
and depending on the cost of the posterboard can be
somewhat expensive but compared to the thrill and
excitement you and your child will have doing math
together it should be worth your effort.

We include here a letter from one of our mothers which states it precisely:

---

22 March

Re: Math Cards

Dear Glenn,

Dots are terrific! I don't know what I am doing but the kids love it.

However, I just thought you'd like to know that my cost for the set of 100 cards was:

$16.50	Canadian $s for dots
$15.00	posterboard at 10% discount
$10.00	vinyl covering at 1/3 the
————	regular price which equals
$41.50	plus ? hours of cross-eyed work.

Can't really recommend that to my friends! When are you planning to sell a ready-made set?

Mrs. van Arragon
Ontario, Canada

P.S. Please hurry with your book. I need help.

As a result of this sound parental advice, there is a kit now available with these cards already made up for parents.

These first one hundred cards are all you need to begin step one of your math program. Once you begin to teach your child mathematics you will find that your child goes through new material very quickly. No matter how often we emphasize this point with parents, they are always astonished at how quickly their children learn.

We discovered a long time ago that it is best to start out ahead. For this reason, make all one hundred dot cards before you actually begin to teach your child. Then you will have an adequate supply of new material on hand and ready to use. If you do not do this, you will find yourself constantly behind. The temptation to keep showing the same old cards over and over again looms large. If mother succumbs to this temptation it spells disaster for her math program. The one mistake a child will not tolerate is to be shown the same material over and over again long after it should have been retired.

Remember the cardinal sin is to bore the tiny child.

Be smart—start ahead in material preparation and stay ahead. And if for some reason you do get behind in preparing new materials, do not fill in the gap by showing the same old cards again. Stop your program for a day or a week until you have reorganized and made new material, then begin again where you left off.

Material preparation can be a lot of fun and should be. If you are preparing next month's materials, it will be. If you are preparing tomorrow morning's materials it will not be.

Start out ahead, stay ahead, stop and reorganize if you must, but don't show old materials over and over again.

Summary: The Basics of Good Teaching

1. Begin as young as possible.
2. Be joyous at all times.
3. Respect your child.
4. Teach only when you and your child are happy.
5. Stop before your child wants to stop.
6. Show materials quickly.
7. Introduce new materials often.
8. Do your program consistently.
9. Prepare your materials carefully and stay ahead.
10. Remember the Fail-Safe Law:
    If you aren't having a wonderful time and your child isn't having a wonderful time— stop. You are doing something wrong.

8

How to Teach
Quantity Recognition

THE MATH PATHWAY

The path that you will now follow in order to teach your child is amazingly simple and easy. Whether you are beginning with an infant or an eighteen-month-old the path is essentially the same.

The steps of that path are as follows:

First Step	Quantity Recognition
Second Step	Equations
Third Step	Problem Solving
Fourth Step	Numeral Recognition
Fifth Step	Equations with numerals

THE FIRST STEP (*Quantity Recognition*)

Your first step is teaching your child to be able to perceive actual numbers, which are the true value of numerals. Numerals, remember, are merely symbols to represent the true value of numbers. You will begin by teaching your baby (at the youngest age possible down to birth) the dot cards from one to ten. You will begin with cards one to five.

Begin at a time of day when your child is receptive, rested and in a good mood.

Use a part of the house with as few distracting factors as possible, in both an auditory and a visual sense; for instance, do *not* have the radio playing and avoid other sources of noise. Use a corner of a room that does not have a great deal of furniture, pictures, or other objects that might distract your child visually.

Now the fun begins. Simply hold up the "one card" just beyond his reach and say to him clearly and enthusiastically, "This is one." Show it to him very briefly, no longer than it takes to say it. One second or less.

Give your child no more description. There is no need to elaborate.

Next, hold up the "two card" and again with great enthusiasm say, "This is two."

Show the three, four, and five card in precisely the same way as you have the first two cards. It is best when showing a set of cards to take the card from the back of the set rather than feeding from the front card. This allows you to glance at one of the corners of the back of the card where you have written the number. This means that as you actually say the number to your child you can put your full attention on his face. This is ideal because you want to have your full attention and enthusiasm directed toward him rather than looking at the card as he looks at it.

Remember the more quickly you show him the cards the better his attention and interest will be. Remember also that your child will have had your happy and undivided attention and there is nothing that a tiny child loves more than that.

Do not ask your child to repeat the numbers as you go along. After the five card has been shown give your child a huge hug and kiss and display your affection in the most obvious ways. Tell him how wonderful and bright he is and how much you love teaching him.

Repeat this two more times during the first day, in exactly the manner described above. In the first few weeks of your math program sessions should be at least one half-hour apart. After that, sessions can be fifteen minutes apart.

The first day is now over and you have taken the first step in teaching your child to understand mathematics. (You have thus far invested at most three minutes.)

The second day, repeat the basic session three times. Add a second set of five new dot cards (six, seven, eight, nine, and ten). This new set should be seen three times throughout the day. Since you now

will be showing two sets of five cards and each set
will be taught three times in the day you will be
doing a total of six math sessions daily.

The very first time you teach the set of cards from
one to five and the set of cards from six to ten you
may show them in order (i.e. one, two, three, four,
five). After that initial showing *make sure that you
always shuffle each set of cards before the next
showing so that the sequence in which your child
will see the cards is unpredictable.*

At the end of each session tell your child he is
very good and very bright. Tell him that you are
very proud of him and that you love him very much.
It is wise to hug him and to express your love for
him physically.

Do not bribe him or reward him with cookies,
candy, or the like. At the rate he will be learning in
a very short time, you will not be able to afford
enough cookies from a financial standpoint and he
will not be able to afford them from a health standpoint. Besides, cookies are a meager reward for
such a major accomplishment, compared with your
love and respect.

Children learn at lightning speed—if you show
them the math cards more than three times a day
you will bore them. If you show your child a single
card for more than a second you will lose him. Try
an experiment with his dad. Ask Dad to stare at a
card with six dots on it for thirty seconds. You'll find
that he'll have great difficulty in doing so. Remember that babies perceive much faster than grown-
ups.

Now you are teaching your child two sets of math cards with five cards in each set, each set three times a day. You and your child are now enjoying a total of six math sessions spread out during the day, equaling a few minutes in all.

The only warning sign in the entire process of learning math is boredom. *Never bore the child. Going too slowly is much more likely to bore him than going too quickly.* Remember that this bright baby can be learning, say, Portuguese at this time, so don't bore him. Consider the splendid thing you have just accomplished. You have given your child the opportunity to learn the true quantity of ten when he is actually young enough to perceive it. This is an opportunity you and I never had. He has done, with your help, two most extraordinary things:

1. His visual pathway has grown and, more important, he is able to differentiate between one quantity or value and another.
2. He has mastered something that we adults are unable to do and, in all likelihood, never will do.

Continue to show the two sets of five cards but after the second day mix the two sets up so that one set might be three, ten, eight, two and five while the remaining cards would be in the other set. This constant mixing and reshuffling will help to keep each session exciting and new. Your child will never know which number is going to come up next. This is a very important part of keeping your teaching fresh and interesting.

Continue to teach these two sets of five cards in this way for five days. On the sixth day you will begin to add new cards and put away old cards.

Here is the method you should use from this point on in adding new cards and taking out old ones: simply remove the two lowest numbers from the ten cards you have been teaching for five days. In this case you would remove the one card and the two card and replace those cards with two new cards (eleven and twelve). From this point on you should add two new cards daily and put away two old cards. We call this process of putting away an old card "retirement." However every retired card will later be called back to active duty when we get to the second and third steps as you will see shortly.

DAILY PROGRAM
(after the first day)

Daily Content:	2 sets
One Session:	1 set (5 cards) shown once
Frequency:	3 x daily each set
Intensity:	3/4-inch red dots
Duration:	5 seconds per session
New Cards:	2 daily (1 in each set)
Retired Cards:	2 daily (two lowest)
Life Span of Each Card:	3 x daily for 5 days = 15 x
Principle:	Always stop before your child wants to stop.

In summary, you will be teaching ten cards daily, divided into two sets of five cards each. Your child will be seeing two new cards daily or one new card for each set and the two lowest cards will be retired each day.

Children who have already been taught to count from one to ten or higher may attempt to count each card at first. Knowing how to count causes minor confusion to the child. He will be gently discouraged from doing this by the speed at which the cards are shown. Once he realizes how quickly the cards are shown, he will see that this is a different game from the counting games he is used to playing and should begin to learn to recognize the quantities of dots that he is seeing. For this reason if your tiny child does not know how to count, do not introduce this until *well after* he has completed steps one through five of this pathway.

Again one must remember the supreme rule of never boring the child. If he is bored there is a strong likelihood that you are going too slowly. He should be learning quickly and pushing you to play the game some more.

If you have done it well he will be averaging two new cards daily. This is actually a *minimum* number of new cards to introduce daily. You may feel that he needs new material more quickly. In this case, you should retire three cards daily and add three new ones or even four.

By now both parent and child should be approaching the math game with great pleasure and anticipation. Remember, you are building into your child a love of learning that will multiply throughout his life. More accurately, you are reinforcing a built-in rage for learning that will not be denied but which can certainly be twisted into useless or even negative channels in a child. Play the game with joy and enthusiasm. You have spent no more than three minutes teaching him and five or six loving him and he has made one of the most important discoveries he will ever make in his whole life.

Indeed, if you have given him this knowledge eagerly and joyously and as a pure gift with no demands of repayment on the child's part, he will have already learned what few adults in history have ever learned. He will actually be able to *perceive* what you can only *see*. He will actually be able to distinguish thirty-nine dots from thirty-eight dots or ninety-one dots from ninety-two dots. He now knows *true* value and not merely symbols and has the basis he needs to truly understand math and not merely memorize formulas and rituals such as "I put down the 6 and carry the 9." He will now be able to recognize at a glance forty-seven dots, forty-seven pennies, or forty-seven sheep.

If you have been able to resist testing, he may now have demonstrated his ability by accident. In either case, trust him a bit longer. Don't be misled into believing he can't do math this way merely because you've never met an adult who could. Neither could any of them learn English as fast as every kid does.

You continue to teach the dot cards, in the way described here, all the way up to one hundred. It is not necessary to go beyond one hundred with the quantity cards, although a few zealous parents have done so over the years. After one hundred you are only playing with zeros. Once your child has seen the dot cards from one to one hundred he will have a very fine idea of quantity.

In fact, he will need and want to begin on the second step of the Math Pathway well *before* you get all the way up to one hundred in the dots. When you have completed one to twenty with the dot cards it is time to begin the second step.

9

How to Teach
Equations

THE SECOND STEP (*Equations*)

By this time your child will have quantity recognition from one to twenty. At this point there is sometimes the temptation to review old cards over and over again. Resist this temptation. Your child will find this boring. Children love to learn new numbers but they do not love to go over and over old ones. You may also be tempted to test your child. Again, do not do this. Testing invariably introduces tension into the situation on the part of the parent and children perceive this readily. They are likely to associate tension and unpleasantness with learning. We will discuss testing in greater detail later in the book.

Be sure to show your child how much you love and respect him at every opportunity.

Math sessions should always be a time of laughter and physical affection. They become the perfect reward for you and your child.

Once a child has acquired a basic recognition of quantity from one to twenty, he is ready to begin to put some of these quantities together to see what other quantities result. He is ready to begin addition.

The process of beginning to teach addition equations is very easy. In fact, your child has already been watching the process for several weeks.

Every time you showed him a new dot card he has seen the addition of one new dot. This process becomes so predictable to the tiny child that it is clear he begins to anticipate cards he has not yet seen. However, he has no way of predicting or deducing *the name* we have given the condition of "twenty-one." He has probably deduced that the new card we are going to show him is going to look exactly like twenty except it is going to have *one more dot on it.*

This of course is called addition. He doesn't know what it is called yet but he does have a rudimentary idea about what it is and how it works. It is important to understand that he will have reached this point *before* you actually begin to show him addition equations for the first time.

You can prepare your materials by simply writing two-step addition equations on the backs of your cards in pencil or pen. A few moments with your calculator and you can put quite a number on the back of each dot card from one to twenty. In the appendix of this book you will find some equations to get you started. For example the back of your ten card should look like this:

```
10                                                10

       1 + 9 = 10                    100 ÷ 10 = 10
       2 + 8 = 10                     70 ÷ 7 = 10
       3 + 7 = 10                     40 ÷ 4 = 10
       4 + 6 = 10                     30 ÷ 3 = 10
       5 + 5 = 10                     20 ÷ 2 = 10


       100 − 90 = 10
       80 − 70 = 10                   15 − 5 = 10
       30 − 20 = 10                   16 − 6 = 10
       20 − 10 = 10                   17 − 7 = 10
       1 + 2 + 3 + 4 = 10             18 − 8 = 10
                                      19 − 9 = 10
10                                                10
```

To begin this process place on your lap face down the one, two and three cards. Using a happy and enthusiastic tone simply say "One plus two equals three." As you say this you show the card for the number you are saying.

Therefore for this particular equation you hold up

the one card and say "one" (put down the one card) and say "plus" (pick up the two card) and say "two" (put down the two card) and say "equals" (pick up the three card) and say " three".

He learns what the word "plus" and the word "equals" mean in the same way he learns what the words "mine" and "yours" mean, which is by seeing them in action and in context.

This should be done very quickly and naturally. Again practice on Dad a few times until you feel comfortable. The trick here is to have the equation set up and ready to go before you draw your child's attention to the fact that a math session is about to begin. It is foolish to expect your baby to sit and watch you shuffle around for the correct card to make the equation that you are about to show him. He will simply creep away and he should. His time is valuable too.

Set up the sequence of your equation cards for next day *the night before* so that when a good time presents itself you are ready to go. Remember you will not be staying on the simple equations of one to twenty for long, soon you will be doing equations that you can not do in your head so readily or so accurately.

Each equation takes only a few seconds to show. Don't try to explain what "plus" or "equals" means. It is not necessary because you are doing something far better than explaining what they mean you are demonstrating what they are. Your child is actually seeing the process rather than merely hearing about it. The simple action of showing the equation defines clearly what "plus" means and what "equals" means. This is teaching at its best.

If someone says, "One plus two equals three" to an adult, what he sees in his mind's eye is 1 + 2 = 3. Because we adults are limited to seeing the symbols rather than the fact.

What the child is seeing is:

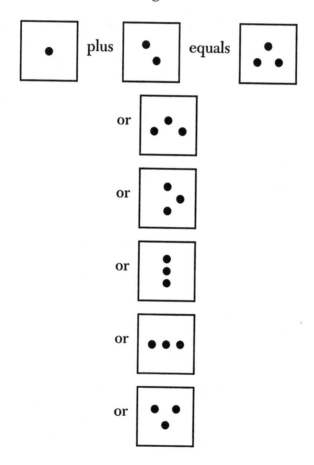

—as all being three. Tiny children see the fact and not the symbol.

Always be consistent about the way you say the equations. Use the same words each time. Say, "One plus two equals three". Don't say, "One and two makes three." When you teach children the facts, they will deduce the rules but we adults must be consistent in order for them to deduce the rules. If we change the vocabulary we use, children have a right to believe that the rules have changed also.

Each session should consist of three equations— no more. You may do less than this but do not do more. Remember you always want to keep the sessions brief.

Do three equation sessions daily. Each of these three sessions will contain three different equations, therefore you will be doing *nine different equations daily*. Please note you do not have to repeat the same equation over and over again. Each day your equations will be new and different from the day before.

Please avoid doing predictable patterns of equations in one session. For example:

```
1 + 2 = 3
1 + 3 = 4
1 + 5 = 6
etc.
```

A much better session would be:

$$
\begin{aligned}
1 + 2 &= 3 \\
2 + 5 &= 7 \\
4 + 8 &= 12
\end{aligned}
$$

It is best to keep the addition equations to two steps because this keeps the session very zippy and crisp, which is much better for the tiny child.

There are 190 different two-step addition equations that can be made using the cards between one and twenty, so don't be afraid that you will run out of ideas in the first week. You have more than enough material here with which to work.

In fact after two weeks of nine different addition equations daily it is time to move on to subtraction or you will lose the attention and interest of your child. He has a very clear idea about adding dots, now he is ready to see them subtracted.

The process you will use to teach subtraction is exactly the same as the process you have used to teach addition. This is the exact method by which he learns English.

Prepare your dot cards by writing various equations on the back. Begin by saying, "Three minus two equals one." Again you will have the three cards that make up each equation on your lap and you will show each card as you say the number:

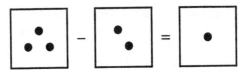

By now you will have gone beyond twenty in teaching the dot cards so you will have an even wider selection of numbers to use to make subtraction equations and you should feel free to use these higher numbers as well.

Now you can stop doing addition equations and replace these sessions with subtraction equations. At this point then you will be doing three subtraction equation sessions daily with three different equations in each session while you are simultaneously continuing two sets of five dot cards three times daily in order to teach the higher numbers up to one hundred. This gives you nine very brief math sessions in a day:

DAILY PROGRAM

Session 1	Dot Cards
Session 2	Subtraction Equations
Session 3	Dot Cards
Session 4	Dot Cards
Session 5	Subtraction Equations
Session 6	Dot Cards
Session 7	Dot Cards
Session 8	Subtraction Equations
Session 9	Dots Cards

Each of these equations has the great virtue that the child knows both quantities:

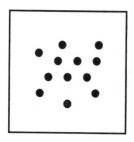

and their names ("twelve") beforehand. The equation contains two basic elements that are satisfying to the child. One aspect that he enjoys is seeing old dot cards he already knows. The second element is that although he already knows these two quantities he now sees that his two old quantities subtracted create a new idea. This is exciting to him. It opens the door for understanding the magic of mathematics.

During the next two weeks you will be majoring in subtraction. During this time you will show approximately 126 different subtraction equations to your child. That is plenty. You do not have to do every possible combination. Now it is time to move on to multiplication.

Multiplication is nothing more than repeated addition so it will not come as any great revelation to your child when you show him his first multiplication equation. He will, however, be learning more of the language of mathematics and this will be very helpful to him.

Since your child's repertoire of dot cards has been growing daily you now have even higher numbers that you can use in your multiplication equations. Not a moment too soon because you will need higher numbers now to supply answers to these equations. Prepare your cards by writing as many multiplication equations as possible on the back of each dot card.

Using three cards say, "Two multiplied by three equals six .":

He will learn what the word "multiplied" means in exactly the same way that he learned what the words "plus," "equals," "minus," "mine," and "yours" mean, by seeing them in action.

Now your subtraction equation sessions will be replaced by multiplication equation sessions. You will do three sessions daily with three different equations in each session. Follow exactly the same pattern you have been following with addition and subtraction. Meanwhile continue the dot card sessions with higher and higher numbers.

Under ideal circumstances your tiny child has seen only *real numbers* in the form of dot cards and has not, as yet, seen any numeral, not even 1 or 2.

The next two weeks are devoted to multiplication. Continue to avoid predictable patterns in the equations that you do in one session, such as

$$2 \times 3 = 6$$
$$2 \times 4 = 8$$
$$2 \times 5 = 10$$

These patterns do have a value—later in the book we will touch upon when to bring them to the attention of your child but not just yet. For the moment we want to keep the tiny child wondering what is coming next. The question, "What's next ?" is the hallmark of the tiny child and each session should provide him with a new and different solution to that mystery.

You and your child have been enjoying math together for less than two months and you have already covered quantity recognition from one to one hundred, addition, subtraction, and multiplication. Not bad for the small investment of time required to do so and the excitement and adventure of learning the language of mathematics.

We have said that you have now completed all the dot cards but this is not quite true. There is actually one quantity card left to teach. We have saved it until last because it is a special one and particularly beloved of tiny children.

It has been said that it took ancient mathematicians five thousand years to invent the idea of zero.

Whether that is the case or not, it may not surprise you to learn that once tiny children discover the idea of quantity they immediately see the need for no quantity.

Little children adore zero and our adventure through the world of real quantity would not be complete without including a zero dot card. This one is very easy to prepare. It is simply an 11" by 11" piece of white posterboard with no dots on it.

The zero dot card will be a hit every time. You will now use the zero card to show your child addition, subtraction and multiplication equations. For example:

Now we have, in fact, completed teaching all the real number cards that we need. However, we are not finished with the dot cards. We will still be using them in many ways to introduce new mathematical ideas as we go along.

After two weeks of multiplication it is time to move on to division. Since your child has completed all the dot cards from zero to one hundred you may use all these cards as the basis for your division equations. Prepare your cards by writing two-step division equations on the backs of many if not all of your one hundred dot cards. (This is a great job for the resident mathematician. If you don't happen to have one, try using Dad.)

Now you simply say to your child, "Six divided by two equals three ."

He will learn what the word "divided" means exactly as he learned what every other word means. Each session contains three different equations. You do three sessions daily so you will cover nine different division equations daily. By now this will be very easy indeed for you and your child.

When you have spent two weeks on division equations you will have fully completed the second step and will be ready to begin the third step on the pathway.

10

How to Teach Problem-Solving

If up to now you have been extraordinarily giving and completely non-demanding, then you are doing very well and you haven't done any testing.

We have said much about teaching but absolutely nothing about testing.

Our strongest advice on this subject is do *not* test your child. Babies love to learn but they hate to be tested. In that way they are very like grown-ups. Testing is the opposite of learning. It is full of stress. To teach a child is to give him a delightful gift. To test him is to demand payment in advance. The more you test him, the slower he will learn and the less he will want to. The less you test him, the quicker he will learn and the more he will want to learn. Knowledge is the most precious gift you can give your child. Give it as generously as you give him food.

What is a test?

In essence it is an attempt to find out what the child *doesn't* know. It is putting him on the spot by saying, "Can you tell the answer to this equation to your father?"

It is essentially disrespectful of the child because he gets the notion that we do not believe he can do math unless he proves it over and over again.

The intention of the test is a negative one—it is to expose what the child does not know.

The result of testing is to decrease learning and the *willingness* to learn. Do not test your child and do not allow anyone else to do so either.

Well what is a mother to do? She does not want to test her child, she wants to teach him and give him every opportunity to experience the joy of learning and accomplishment.

Therefore, instead of testing her child she provides problem-solving opportunities.

The purpose of a problem-solving opportunity is for the child to be able to demonstrate what he knows if he wishes to do so.

It is exactly the *opposite* of the test.

Now you are ready not to *test* him but to *teach* him that he knows how to solve problems (and you'll learn that he can).

A very simple problem-solving opportunity would

be to hold up two dot cards. Let's say you choose "fifteen" and "thirty-two" and you hold them up and ask, "Where is thirty-two? "

This is a good opportunity for a baby to look at or touch the card if he wishes to do so. If your baby looks at the card with thirty-two dots on it or touches it, you are naturally delighted and make a great fuss. If he looks at the other card simply say, "This is thirty-two" and, "This is fifteen."

You're happy, enthusiastic, and relaxed. If he does not respond to your question, hold the card with thirty-two dots a little closer to him and say, "This is thirty-two, isn't it?" again in a happy, enthusiastic, relaxed way. End of opportunity. No matter how he responds, he wins and so do you, because the chances are good that if you are happy and relaxed he will enjoy doing this with you.

These problem-solving opportunities can be put at the end of equation sessions. This creates a nice balance of give and take to the session since each session begins with you giving three equations to your child and ends with an opportunity for your child to solve one equation if he wishes to do so.

You will find that merely giving your child an opportunity to choose one number from another is all right to begin with but you should very shortly move on to opportunities to choose answers to equations. This is a lot more exciting for your child, not to mention for you.

To present these problem-solving opportunities you need the same three cards you would need to show any equation plus a fourth card to use as a choice card. *Don't ask your child to say answers* always give him a choice of two possible answers. Very young children do not speak or are just beginning to speak. Problem-solving situations which demand an oral response will be very difficult if not impossible for them. Even children who are beginning to speak do not like to answer orally (which is in itself another test) so always give your child a choice of answers.

Remember that you are not trying to teach your child to talk, you are teaching him mathematics. He will find choosing to be very easy and a lot of fun, but he will quickly become irritated if we demand speech.

Since you have completed all the dot cards now and addition, subtraction, multiplication, and division at the initial stages you can make your equation sessions even more sophisticated and varied. Continue to do three equation sessions daily. Continue to show three completely different equations at each session. But now it is unnecessary to show all three cards in the equation. Now you need only show the answer card.

This will make the sessions even faster and easier. You simply say, "Twenty-two divided by eleven equals two" and show the "two" card as you say the answer. It is as simple as that.

Your child already knows "twenty-two" and "eleven" so there is no real need to keep showing him the whole equation. Strictly speaking there is no real need to show him the answer either, but we have found that it is helpful for us adults to use visual aids when we teach. The kids seem to prefer it also.

Now the equation sessions will be composed of a variety of equations, for example an addition equation, a subtraction equation, and a division equation.

Now would also be a good time to move on to three-step equations and see if your child enjoys them. If you move quickly enough through the material the chances are very good that he will.

Simply sit down with a calculator and create one or two three step equations for each card and write them clearly on the back of each one. A typical session at this point would be:

Equations:	$2 \times 2 \times 3 = 12$
	$2 \times 2 \times 6 = 24$
	$2 \times 2 \times 9 = 36$
Problem-Solving:	$2 \times 2 \times 12 = ?$
	48 or 52

Please note that these sessions continue to be very, very brief. Your child now has nine three-step equations daily with one problem-solving opportunity tagged on to each session.

Therefore you are giving him the answer to the first three equations in each session and, at the end of each session, giving him the opportunity to choose the answer to the fourth equation if he wishes to do so.

After a few weeks of these equations it is time to add a little additional spice to your sessions again. Now you are going to give your child the type of equations which he will like the best of all.

Begin to use equations which combine addition and subtraction, or multiplication and division. This will introduce your child to two fascinating facts: 1) addition and subtraction are variations of a single operation, and 2) multiplication and division are also only variations of a single operation.

Subtraction of any number is really only the addition of the negative of that number. For example, subtracting 3 from 7 is the same as adding negative 3 to 7. Division by any number is really only multiplication by the inverse of that number. For example, dividing 30 by 5 is the same as multiplying 30 by one fifth.

These are not laws you will explicitly teach your child at this stage of the Math Pathway. They will be covered in good time. What you are doing now is laying the foundation for that later learning, so that when it comes up it will be taken in easily, as it will fit perfectly with the material you are teaching now.

As you take this new step, you can also give your child an opportunity to explore patterns by creating groups of equations that are related by some common element. For example:

$$40 + 15 - 30 = 25$$
$$40 + 15 - 20 = 35$$
$$40 + 15 - 10 = 45$$

or

```
7 + 15 + 8 = 30
7 + 8 + 15 = 30
15 + 8 + 7 = 30
```

or

```
4 × 3 × 5 = 60
3 × 5 × 4 = 60
5 × 3 × 4 = 60
```

or

```
6 × 14 ÷ 2 = 42
6 ÷ 2 × 14 = 42
14 ÷ 2 × 6 = 42
```

Your child will surely find these relationships and patterns interesting, just as all mathematicians do.

There is one important caution. Be careful not to mix these two basic operations: addition/subtraction with multiplication/division. Serious errors can result, errors which can be avoided only after learning both the rule about the Order of Operations AND the reasons behind it. That comes later in the Math Pathway.

After a few weeks, add another term to the equations you are offering. For example:

```
56 + 20 − 4 − 4 = 68
56 + 20 − 8 − 4 = 64
56 + 20 − 16 − 4 = 56
```

That last one should prove particularly enjoyable. These four-step equations are a great deal of fun. If you were a little intimidated at first by the idea of teaching your child mathematics, by now you should be relaxing and really enjoying these more advanced equations just as your child is enjoying them.

From time to time you should feel free to show three unrelated equations as well as those which also teach by the presence of a pattern. For example:

$$100 \div 5 \div 4 \div 5 = 1$$
$$1 + 2 + 3 + 4 + 5 = 15$$
$$80 - 40 - 20 + 60 = 80$$

You will be astonished at the speed at which your child solves equations. You will wonder if he solves them in some psychic way. When adults see two-year-olds solving math problems faster than adults can, they make the following assumptions in the following order:

1. The child is guessing. (The mathematical odds against this, if he is virtually always right, are staggering.)
2. The child isn't actually perceiving the dots but instead is actually recognizing the pattern in which they occur. (Nonsense. He'll recognize the number of men standing in a group, and who can keep people in a pattern? Besides, why can't you recognize the seventy-five pattern on the seventy-five dot card which he knows at a glance?)

3. It's some sort of trick. (You taught him. Did you use any tricks?)
4. The baby is psychic. (Sorry but he isn't: he's just a whiz at learning facts. We'd rather write a book called "How to Make Your Baby Psychic" because that would be even better. Unfortunately we don't know how to make little kids psychic.)

Now the sky is the limit. You can go in many directions with mathematical problem-solving at this point and the chances are extremely good that your child will be more than willing to follow you wherever you decide to go.

For those mothers who would like some further inspiration we include some additional ideas:

1. Sequences
2. Greater than and less than
3. Equalities and inequalities
4. Number personality
5. Fractions
6. Simple algebra

All of these things can be taught using the dot cards and indeed *should* be taught using the dot cards because in this way the child will see the reality of what is truly happening to real quantities rather than learning how to manipulate symbols as we adults were taught.

SEQUENCES

Mathematicians are fascinated by the results of looking at numbers in sequence. The ancient Greek mathematicians found paradoxes in certain kinds of sequences that they never could understand, and some of these relate to the invention of some fields of higher mathematics.

Tiny children, like all other fine mathematicians, love sequences. Introducing your child to sequences that involve only whole numbers is quite easy to do with the dot cards. Begin with those that are the most obvious. For example:

2, 4, 6, 8, 10, 12, 14, 16, 18, 20
5, 10, 15, 20, 25, 30, 35, 40, 45, 50, 55, 60
10, 9, 8, 7, 6, 5, 4, 3, 2, 1, 0

Your child will quickly see, and enjoy, something of the order and pattern in math from seeing such sequences. These first three are what mathematicians call ARITHMETIC PROGRESSIONS. An arithmetic progression can start with any number. They can have any number of terms, finite or infinite, but of course you will be using only finite progressions with your child. These progressions all have a *constant difference,* positive or negative, between successive terms. The constant differences in the three progressions above are two, five, and negative one. You may choose to show all the arithmetic progressions that make up the multiplication tables, forward and backward, and that will surely be helpful to your child when it is time to learn those multiplication facts.

The other principal kind of sequence is called a GEOMETRIC PROGRESSION. In a geometric progression there is a *constant ratio* between successive terms. The following are geometric progressions, with ratios of two, one half, and one third.

1, 2, 4, 8, 16, 32, 64
80, 40, 20, 10, 5
81, 27, 9, 3, 1

Children have an astonishing ability to know what card should come next in the sequence. After you have presented a variety of progressions to your child, you can easily give him a problem-solving opportunity. Simply show the entire sequence as you would normally do and at the end hold you two cards (one is the card that comes next in the sequence and the other is a wild card) and ask, "Which comes next?"

Later in the Math Pathway we will come to more complex progressions. What you do with seqences now will lay the foundation for that kind of further study.

Greater Than and Less Than

Your child certainly already has the idea of greater than and less than; however, he needs to learn the language that mathematicians use in order to describe these conditions. This language can be taught very easily with the dot cards.

You will need to make two new cards. These should be made on 11" by 11" posterboard just like the dot cards. One card will be the "greater than" card and the other the "less than" card. They will look like this:

These sessions will be extremely brief since all you will need is to show three pairs of numbers. A typical pair would be: 25 > 5. Instead of showing one card at a time, as you have been used to do, it is best to sit on the floor and put each card down on the floor as you say it so that your child can see all three cards at one time. As you have been doing, show three pairs in one session. After a few days, include this also as part of problem-solving. You can do this by simply putting down the card 68 and the "greater than" card and asking your child, "Which card goes in this space, 28 or 96?"

Again let him choose one of the two cards to place next to the "greater than" card to answer the question.

EQUALITIES AND INEQUALITIES

Teaching equalities and inequalities is very similar to teaching "greater than" and "less than". You will need six new cards. The math symbol cards are again made on 11" by 11" posterboard cards. Use your large, red felt-tipped marker to make the symbols for addition (+), subtraction (-), multiplication (x), division (÷), equals (=), not equal (≠). Make these figures large, clear and neat so they can be seen easily by your child.

On the back of each one up in the upper left hand corner write in pencil the same symbol. This is for you to know what is on the card as you are showing it to your child. You don't want to have to keep turning the cards around so that you can see what they are when you are teaching your child. This would be distracting and would slow down your sessions.

The cards will look like this:

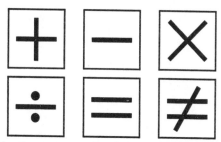

Instead of using single dot cards to show equality and inequality to your child you are going to begin with simple addition and subtraction equations. Some examples would be:

$$2 + 4 \neq 2 + 5$$
$$4 + 5 = 3 + 6$$
$$25 + 4 \neq 25 + 5$$

or

$$8 - 6 \neq 8 - 7$$
$$10 - 3 = 8 - 1$$
$$55 - 10 \neq 50 - 10$$

or

$$3 \times 5 = 5 \times 3$$
$$5 \times 4 \neq 2 \times 12$$
$$5 \times 6 = 10 \times 3$$

or

$$100 \div 50 = 10 \div 5$$
$$20 \div \ 5 \neq 10 \div 2$$
$$5 \div \ 1 = 25 \div 5.$$

It is best to lay these equations out on the floor as you do them, one at a time, so that your child can see the entire equation at one time. As you put down each card on the floor you will say, "Two plus four is *not equal* to two plus five," or, "Four plus five is *equal* to three plus six."

Your child will be learning six vital mathematical symbols which will be very meaningful to him. After all, he has been doing addition, subtraction, multiplication, and division for months now. He will be more than ready to learn these symbols for the first time.

NUMBER PERSONALITIES

As you show the dots, your child may develop a special liking for certain cards. Each arrangement has its own esthetic quality, and a child may respond to that. But beyond that, each number is so special that you might say it has a personality, and your child may be sensing that too. In any case, when you and your child recognize the uniqueness of each number, your ability to handle numbers well will be greatly enhanced.

In the first section, you met some families of

numbers as you looked at sequences: the even numbers, the odd numbers, the multiples of three, and so on. A number may belong to a particularly interesting family, or to several families, and either quality can make it special. Other numbers are what might be called "loners," like 47, belonging to few families.

The number 12 has taken a special place in the history of civilization because it is one of the smallest numbers to be in several very basic families: it is a multiple of 2 and of 3 and of 4. This makes it easy to pack things in dozens, and that is why so many things have been sold by the dozen. Eggs come in cartons arranged 3 by 4, or 2 by 6. Both are convenient.

Two dozen is the number we have chosen for dividing the day up into hours. You can get it by multiplying the first four numbers together: 1 times 2 times 3 times 4. It divides easily into two 12-hour periods, or three 8-hour work shifts, or shorter duty cycles of 6 or 4 or 3 or 2 hours.

Sixty, 5 dozen, is the smallest number to be a member of five very basic families: the multiples of two, three, four, five, and six. This also makes it a multiple of such interesting numbers as 10, 12, 15, 20, and 30. This is why Babylonian mathematics, and later that of the Mayans, was based largely on the number 60. It is also why why divide each hour into 60 minutes, and each minute into 60 seconds.

Some numbers are square. Nine blocks make a square, as in the tic-tac-toe board. The chess board has 64 spaces: another square number. Four, 16, 25,

36, 49, 81 and 100 are other square numbers your child has seen, and he *may* have mentally rearranged the dots on some of those cards into square patterns. Look at egg cartons stacked in the supermarket, and you will see how useful it is that 36 is a square number.

There are other kinds of mental rearranging your child may have done. Some numbers are triangular. Add two pennies to one penny $(1 + 2)$, all flat on a table and all touching each other, and you see a triangle. Add three more in a row under them, and you see that $1 + 2 + 3 + 4 = 10$, making another triangle. Let your child discover the next few in this family. He may notice that 36 is both a triangular number and a square number.

Seven is a hexagonal number. Surround a single penny with six others, all touching it, and you see the pattern. What are some other hexagonal numbers? Can you find a hexagonal number which is also a square number?

Seven is also a member of another very interesting family: the "prime" numbers. Primes are numbers which cannot be arranged in equal rows of any kind. The three smallest primes are 2, 3 and 5. Some children dislike prime numbers; others love them. Sixty, the number the Babylonians and Mayans loved, can be arranged in two rows of 30, three rows of 20, four rows of 15, five rows of 12 or six rows of 10. But prime numbers, numbers like 7 and 11 and 13 cannot be arranged that way. Maybe that is why Betsy Ross arranged the thirteen stars on our first flag in a circle.

You may have noticed the personality of these numbers, and others, showing up in may of the math adventures you and your child have already taken as you worked with equalities, inequalities and operations. Seeing numbers this way can also help as you relate mathematics to everyday life.

In order to begin to have a sense of the personality of a number take one number and concentrate on it until you have exhausted all the possibilities. The number 1 for example:

$1 + 0 = 1$	$2 - 1 = 1$	$2 \div 2 = 1$	$2 \times 1/2 = 1$
$1 \times 1 = 1$	$3 - 2 = 1$	$3 \div 3 = 1$	$3 \times 1/3 = 1$
$1 \div 1 = 1$	$4 - 3 = 1$	$4 \div 4 = 1$	$4 \times 1/4 = 1$
$1 - 0 = 1$	$10 - 9 = 1$	$10 \div 10 = 1$	$5 \times 1/5 = 1$

or the number 12

$12 + 0 = 12$	$13 - 1 = 12$	$2 \times 6 = 12$
$12 \times 1 = 12$	$14 - 2 = 12$	$3 \times 4 = 12$
$12 \div 1 = 12$	$15 - 3 = 12$	$2 \times 2 \times 3 = 12$
$24 - 12 = 12$	$16 - 4 = 12$	
$24 \div 2 = 12$	$3 + 3 + 3 + 3 = 12$	1/2 of $24 = 12$
$36 \div 3 = 12$	$4 + 4 + 4 = 12$	1/3 of $36 = 12$
$48 \div 4 = 12$	$6 + 6 = 12$	1/4 of $48 = 12$
$60 \div 5 = 12$	$10 + 2 = 12$	1/5 of $60 = 12$

In the appendix of this book you will find equations to put on the back of your dot cards to help get you started on this.

As you and your child begin to get into the spirit of really looking at the unique characteristics of each number, your child may want to make his own proposals for equations that equal twelve or whatever number it is that you may be using.

This would be a good point to have pennies or perhaps red poker chips handy. Then you and your child can discover what patterns can be made with twelve.

One session would consist of four related equations such as:

$$1 + 0 = 1$$
$$1 - 0 = 1$$
$$1 \times 1 = 1$$
$$1 \div 1 = 1.$$

Be careful because once you start on this game you will find that you and your child will want to discover all the possibilities for a number. It can be done but not in one session.

Another session would consist of getting out twelve poker chips and experimenting with the different patterns that you or your child can make with twelve.

FRACTIONS

Fractions are also quite easy to introduce with the dot cards. Of course you must choose those fractions which you can show using the zero through one hundred cards, but there are many possibilities. To teach fractions this is all you will need to do. Simply say to your child, "One tenth of ten (showing him the ten card) equals one (showing him the one card)":

1/10 of [●●● / ●● ●● / ● ●● / ●● ●] = [●]

A typical session would be:

```
1/3  of  3  =  1
1/3  of  6  =  2
1/3  of  9  =  3
```

It is as simple as that.

SIMPLE ALGEBRA

Unless mathematics was your favorite subject in school, you probably look back on your final algebra class with fond memories because you believed (as it turns out incorrectly) that you would never have to do algebra again. You will be surprised and delighted to discover that algebra the second time around turns out to be not only easy but a great deal of fun. All you have to do to begin algebra with your tiny child is to introduce the idea of a variable quantity represented by a letter. Often the letter used is "x"; however, since this might easily be confused with the symbol for multiplication, we would recommend that you use "y" instead. The first thing you need to do is make the "y" card on 11" by 11" posterboard. Now you are ready to show your child his first algebra equation. It might be :

$$5 + y = 7$$

You put down the card with five dots on it, then the plus sign, then the y card, the equal sign, then the seven card. You say each of these things as you put down the cards:

Then you pose the question, "What does 'y' stand for ?"

Then you answer the question, "In this equation 'y' stands for two."

Once you have given your child the opportunity to see many of these equations, you can let him help you solve for "y" by putting out two choices and having him choose which answer he thinks is best.

Now that doesn't sound too difficult does it? In fact there are many, many wonderful problem-solving opportunities that you will discover all by yourself as you become reacquainted with mathematics and find that, in fact, you are not as bad a mathematician as you thought you were.

Indeed, maybe you would have been a *great* mathematician if you had had the fine teacher your child now has.

11

How to Teach Numerals

This step is ridiculously easy. We can now begin the process of teaching the numerals or symbols that represent the true values or quantities that your child already knows so well.

You will need to make a set of numeral cards for your child. It is best to make a complete set from zero to one hundred. These should be on 11" by 11" posterboard and the numerals should be made with the large, red, felt-tipped marker. Again you want to make the numerals very large—6" tall and at least 3" wide. Make sure to make your strokes wide so that the numerals are in bold figures.

Be consistent about how you print. Again, your child needs the visual information to be consistent and reliable. This helps him enormously.

Always label your materials on the upper left-hand side. If you do this you will always know that you have them right-side up when you are showing them to your child.

This is not a consideration with the dot cards you have already made to show quantity since there *is* no right-side up or upside down to those cards. In fact, you want to show those cards every which way they come up—that is why on the back of the dot cards you have labeled all four corners not just the upper left-hand corner.

On the back of the numeral cards, print the numeral again in the upper left-hand corner. Make this whatever size is easy for you to see and read. You may use pencil or pen to do this.

Your numeral cards should look like this:

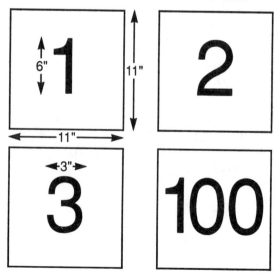

Sometimes mothers get very fancy and use stencils to make their cards. This makes very beautiful numeral cards; however, the time involved is prohibitive. Your time is precious. Mothers have to budget time more carefully than members of almost any other profession. You need to develop a fast, efficient means of making your math cards because you are going to need *a lot* of them in the future.

Neatness and legibility are far more important than perfection. Often mothers find that fathers can make very nice cards and that they appreciate having a hand in the math program.

At this stage in your daily program you are doing three sessions a day of equations with a bit of problem-solving at the end of each of those sessions, but you have long since finished the six sessions you used to do in order to teach the dot cards initially. Now you will teach the numeral cards in exactly the same way that you taught the dot cards several months ago.

You will have two sets of numeral cards with five cards in each set. Begin with 1 to 5 and 6 to 10. You may show them in order the first time but after that always shuffle the cards so that the sequence is unpredictable. As before, each day retire the two lowest numerals and add the next two. Make sure that each set being shown has a new card in it every day rather than one set having two new cards and the other set remaining the same as the day before.

Show each of the sets three times daily. Please note that your child may learn these cards incredibly quickly so be prepared to go even faster if necessary.

If you find that you are losing your child's attention and interest, speed up the introduction of new material. Instead of retiring two cards daily, retire three or four cards and put in three or four new cards. At this point you may find that three times daily is too high a frequency. If your child is interested during the first two sessions each day but consistently creeps away for the third session then drop the frequency from three times daily to two times daily.

You must at all times be sensitive to your child's attention, interest, and enthusiasm. These elements when carefully observed by you will be invaluable tools in shaping and reshaping your child's daily program to suit his needs as he changes and develops.

At the very most it should take you no longer than fifty days to complete all the numerals from zero to one hundred. In all likelihood it will take a lot less time than this.

Once you have reached the numeral 100 you should feel free to begin to show a variety of numerals higher than 100. Your child will be thrilled to see numerals for 200, 300, 400, 500, and 1,000. After this come back and show him examples of 210, 325, 450, 586, 1,830. Don't feel that you must show each and every numeral under the sun. This would bore your child tremendously. You have already taught him the basics of numeral recognition by doing zero to one hundred. Now be adventurous and give him a taste of a wide diet of numerals.

When you have taught the numerals from zero to twenty it is time to begin a bridging step of relating the symbols to the dots. There are a multitude of ways of doing this. One of the easiest ways is to go back to equalities, inequalities, greater than, and less than and use dot cards and symbol cards together.

Take the dot card for ten and put it on the floor, then put down the not equal sign, then the numeral card 35 and say, "Ten is not equal to thirty-five."

One session would look like this:

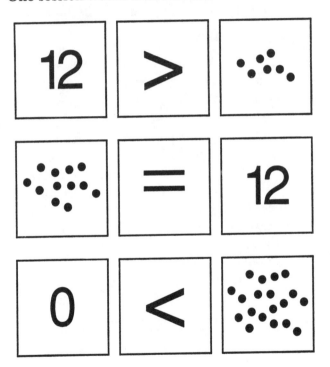

As you work your way up through the numeral cards play this game with as many numeral cards and dots cards as you have the time and inclination to do.

Children also like to join in and choose their own combinations using the dot cards and the numeral cards.

Learning the numerals is a very simple step for your child. Do it quickly and joyously so you can get on to the fifth step as soon as possible.

THE FIFTH STEP (*Equations with numerals*)

The fifth step is really a repetition of all that has come before. It recapitulates the entire process of addition, subtraction, multiplication, division, sequences, equalities, inequalities, greater than, less than, square roots, fractions, and simple algebra.

Now you will need a good supply of posterboard cut into strips 18" long and 4" wide. These cards will be used to make equation cards using numerals. At this stage we recommend that you switch from using red to black felt-tipped marker. The numerals you will be writing now will be smaller than before and black has greater contrast than red for these smaller figures. Your numerals should be 2" tall and 1" wide.

Your first cards would look like this:

Now go back to Step Two of the pathway and follow the instructions, only this time using new equation cards with numerals instead of the dot cards. When you have completed Step Two go on to Step Three.

For Step Three you will need to make some materials suitable for problem-solving opportunities. Now make a quantity of cards to use which do not have answers written on them. Again use single numeral cards to provide your child with choice cards. It will be helpful to you if you always write the correct answer on the top left hand corner of these problem-solving cards along with the problem itself so that you are never at a loss to know what the answer really is:

$$25 + 5$$

25 + 5 = 30

(reverse)

Here are some examples of what your materials will look like as you work your way through the operations that you have already done with dots:

Subtraction Equations

$$30 - 12 = 18$$

$$98 - 2 - 10 = 86$$

$$100 - 23 - 70 \neq 0$$

Multiplication Equations

$$3 \times 5 = 15$$

$$14 \times 2 \times 3 = 84$$

$$115 \times 3 \times 2 \times 5 \neq 2,500$$

Division

$$84 \div 28 = 3$$

$$192 \div 6 \div 8 = 4$$

$$96 \div 12 = 8$$

$$458 \div 2 = 229$$

Continue to use these 2" size numerals long enough to be sure that your child is comfortable with this size. When this part of your program is going smoothly you can begin the process of making the numerals smaller. This must be a gradual process. If you make your numerals too small too quickly you will lose the attention and interest of your child.

When you have gradually reduced the numeral size to one inch or smaller you will have more space on the cards to write longer and more sophisticated equations. As part of your problem-solving program at this point your child may wish to choose numerals and operational symbols (=, ≠, +, -, x, ÷) and make his own equations for you to answer. Keep your calculator handy you will be needing it!

SUMMARY

When you have completed the first through the fifth steps of the Math Pathway you will have reached the end of the beginning of your child's lifelong adventure in mathematics. He will have had a superbly joyous introduction into the world of arithmetic. He will have mastered four basic but vital truths in mathematics.

First, he will have learned about quantity. Indeed he will be able to differentiate many different quantities from one another.

Second, he will have learned how to put those quantities together and take those quantities apart. He will literally have seen hundreds of different combinations and permutations of quantities.

Third, he will have learned that there are symbols that we use to represent the reality of each of the quantities and how to read those symbols.

And finally and most important, he will know the difference between the reality of quantity and the symbols that have arbitrarily been chosen to represent those quantities.

Arithmetic will be the end of the beginning for him because he will now easily and happily be able to make the leap from the simple mechanics of arithmetic to the much more fascinating and creative world of higher mathematics. This is a world of thinking and reasoning and logic, not merely predictable calculations but instead a genuine adventure where new things are discovered all the time.

Sadly this is a world that very few have ever entered. The vast majority of us escaped from mathematics at the earliest possible moment and long before the exciting world of higher mathematics was in view. Indeed it has always been considered a closed shop where only a lucky few gain entrance. Instead of arithmetic being a springboard to higher mathematics, it closed the doors to this wonderful language.

Every child should have the right to master this superb language. You will have bought your child his passport.

12

The Perfect Age
to Begin

He can't learn any younger

—William Ricker
1890

You now understand the basic steps in the Math Pathway. These steps apply regardless of the age of your child. However, how you actually begin with your child and which steps may need to be emphasized will depend upon the age of your child when you begin your math program.

The pathway we have just described is the pathway to follow and it works. However, it is to be remembered that a newborn is in no way the same person as a two-year-old.

The steps of the pathway do not change, regardless of the child's age and the sequence of the steps of the pathway remains the same regardless of the child's age.In this chapter we will outline the refinements and nuances that will enhance your math program and enable you to succeed more easily no matter what age your baby may be when you begin your program.

At this point there may be a temptation to read and study only the section pertaining to your child at this moment. However, it is important to understand all of the points covered in each section so that as your child grows and develops you understand how to change and reshape his program.

The Newborn Child

It is important to know if you intend to start at birth, that at first your program is not a math program—it is really a program of visual stimulation.

In the context of our Math Pathway the newborn child needs the step before the *first step*. We shall call this the *zero step* because before he can truly be ready for the *first step* of his mathematics program he needs the *zero step*, which is a program of visual stimulation.

At birth your baby can see only light and dark. He cannot yet see detail. Within the first few hours or days of life he will begin to see outlines poorly for brief periods. As his ability to see outlines is stimulated by opportunities to see outlines all around him he will begin for *very* brief periods to see detail poorly. By very brief periods we mean a few seconds. At this stage, seeing outline is an effort for a newborn. Seeing detail is a monumental effort.

However, it is an effort he is willing to make because his need to see is so strong.

Newborns begin to see the dark shape of Mother's head moving in front of the light of a sunny window. The more opportunity the infant has to see this contrast of a stable black outline on a well-lighted background the better his vision becomes.

Once he can see outline, he begins to search for detail within the outline. Mother's eyes, nose or mouth are the details he sees first.

It is not within the scope of this book to describe in detail the growth and development of the visual pathway of the newborn baby. However, showing a tiny infant quantity cards does play an important part in stimulating and developing the ability to see detail. *This ability is a result of stimulation and opportunity. It is* **not** *a matter of some preset hereditary alarm clock ringing and causing it to happen, as has been previously believed.*

The newborn who is presented with opportunity to see outline and detail will develop these abilities more quickly and thus will graduate more quickly from being functionally blind, as he is at birth, to being able to see well without effort.

This visual stimulation program is extremely easy and, when you think about it, totally logical. After all, you are talking to your baby at birth. Indeed, have you not been talking to him for the nine months prior to his delivery?

No one would question the sense of talking to a newborn baby. We all recognize that it is the birthright of every baby to hear his language. And yet spoken language is a wild abstraction. We could say it is no more or less abstract than written language but the truth is that spoken language is actually a good bit harder for the tiny baby to decode than written language. It is a basic tenet of all teaching to be consistent. And yet it is very difficult when using spoken language to be consistent. We are apt to say to the tiny infant, "How are *you* ?" Later we may say, "*How* are you?"And before the day ends, "How *are* you?"

We have said the same thing three times. But is it the same thing?

To the immature auditory pathway of the tiny infant these are three different things; each one has a different emphasis. He is looking for the similarities and the differences between these three questions.

Now consider the advantages of the visual pathway. We take our large white card with three large red dots on it. We hold it up and say, "Three." We show this card many times throughout the day. To the tiny infant, each time he sees the card it looks identical to the card he has seen before. Indeed, it looks the same because it *is* the same. The result is that he learns this much more quickly and easily through his visual pathway than he would have through his auditory pathway.

You should begin with the dot cards. It is best to begin with cards one to seven.

Since you are beginning with a newborn, your first set of dots needs to be *very* large. Use posterboard that is 15" by 15". Your dots should be 1 1/2" in diameter. They can be drawn using circles of this size, or larger if you like, and colored in with a felt-tipped marker. At this point your baby is struggling to see outline, so it is best to make black dots on the white posterboard. These will be easier to see at this stage than the red dots. You need *very bold* dots to get the appropriate intensity for an infant. Remember this is visual stimulation, first and foremost.

If you are starting at birth or shortly thereafter, you will want to begin with one dot card. Begin with the "one" card. While you are cradling your baby in your arms hold the card about eighteen inches from him and say "one." Now hold the card and wait. You will watch him do his best to locate the card. When he does see it, say "one" again loudly and clearly. He will try to focus for a second or two—now put the card away.

Because a tiny infant cannot see outline or detail, there is a temptation to sweep visual information across his field of vision in an attempt to catch his attention.

Remember, he has superb attention but very poor vision. If we sweep the card in front of him, he must attempt to focus on a moving object. This is much more difficult than locating a stationary object. Therefore, you should hold the card absolutely still and give him the time he needs to locate the card. At first it will take ten to fifteen seconds or even longer but each day you will observe a measurable decrease in the time it takes him to locate the card and focus on it briefly.

His ability to locate the card and focus on it will

be a product of how many times we show him the card. Each time it will be a little bit easier than the time before.

It is extremely important to provide excellent lighting. The light should be directed toward the card, never in the eyes of the baby. This lighting needs to be markedly better than what is considered adequate ambient light for you and me.

You will be accelerating and enhancing the incredible process of the development of human vision from the crude ability to see light to the more sophisticated ability to recognize mother's smile from across the room.

On the first day show the "one" card. Show this card ten times that day. If you can show it even more often, that is very good. Many mothers keep their dot cards where they diaper their babies. Each time the baby is changed, mother takes the opportunity to show him his dot card. This works very well.

The second day choose the "two" card and show that ten times. Each day for seven days choose a different dot card and show it ten times in the day. This means that by the end of the week you will have shown card "one" to "seven".

At the beginning of the following week go back to the "one" card and again show it ten times. Repeat this process for three weeks. This will mean, for example, that every Monday the baby will see *the "one" card* ten times.

By now, if you started at birth, your three-week-old baby is definitely able to focus on his dot cards more quickly. In fact, as soon as you pull out a card, he may immediately show signs of excitement and anticipation by wiggling his body and kicking his legs.

When this happens it is a most exciting moment for you because you now realize that your baby is not only seeing but is understanding what he sees and, even more important, he is enjoying the experience tremendously. Each day this program of visual stimulation becomes easier and easier for your baby as his ability to focus and see detail develops.

In the early stages of visual development you will find that your tiny infant's visual ability varies throughout the day. When he is well rested and fed, he will be using his visual abilities constantly but will tire very quickly. When he is sleepy, he will turn off his vision and see very little. When he is hungry, he will put his energy into convincing you to feed him.

Therefore, you must choose the correct time to show him a dot card. You will quickly learn to anticipate his best times and avoid the hungry or sleepy times. Sometimes he may be under the weather for a day or two. This may make him cranky and out of sorts almost all the time. Don't show him dot cards on these days—wait until he is back to his old self.

Then start back exactly where you left off. You do not need to go back and review.

After the first seven dot cards have been repeated for three weeks, choose "eight" through "fourteen" and cycle through them in the same way until your tiny infant is seeing detail consistently and easily. In the average baby who is receiving no organized stimulation this will not happen until twelve weeks or later. In your baby who has had a program of visual stimulation, this may occur between eight to ten weeks.

Mothers are superb at knowing when their infants can see them easily. At this point a tiny baby recognizes mother easily and instantly responds to her smile without needing any auditory or tactile clues. At this point a baby is using his vision almost all the time. It is only during the rare moment of extreme fatigue or illness when he turns off his vision.

You have now fully completed the zero step with your baby and he is ready to graduate to the *first step* because you have actually grown his visual pathway. He is ready to begin on the Math Pathway and to follow the program outlined there (Chapter Seven). Since your baby has already been seeing dot cards "one" through "fourteen" in very large dots for one or two months, you can move right into two groups of five dot cards three times daily.

At this point your program shifts gears from the slow and deliberate visual stimulation program to a very fast-paced math program. Now your baby will develop quantity recognition at an astounding rate just as he is learning language through his ear at an astounding rate.

Starting with an Infant (Three Months to Six Months)

If you are beginning your math program with a three- to six-month-old, he will be *majoring* in the *first and second steps* of the Math Pathway. These steps will be the heart of your program.

The two most important things to remember are:

1. Show the dot cards very quickly.
2. Add new cards often.

The wonderful thing about a *tiny* infant is that he is a pure intellectual. He learns anything with a total impartiality and without any bias whatsoever. He learns for learning's sake, without any strings attached. Of course his survival depends on this characteristic, but it is an admirable characteristic and is no less admirable for being tied to his survival.

He is the kind of intellectual we would all like to be but which very few of us are. He loves everything there is to learn. It is his glory *and* ours if we are lucky enough to have the opportunity to teach him.

Between three months and six months of age a tiny baby is able to take in language at an astounding rate. He is also seeing detail consistently. In short, he is able to absorb spoken language without the slightest difficulty, as long as we make that information *loud* and clear. He is able to absorb written language as long as we make it *large* and clear. It is our objective to keep his math cards large and bold so that the baby can always see them easily.

At this stage a baby is using sounds to talk to us. However it will be months before we are able to decode all these sounds as the words, sentences, and paragraphs that they are. In adult terms, then, the baby cannot talk.

He has superb sensory pathways to take in information but he has not yet developed the motor pathways sufficiently to get information back out in a way that can readily be understood.

Since this is the case, someone will no doubt ask you how you can teach a baby mathematics when he cannot yet talk.

The baby learns mathematics through the use of his visual pathway and his auditory pathway. He does not learn through the use of his own speech— this is out-put. Learning is by definition the process of taking in new information. It is the process of receiving in-put—not producing out-put.

Learning to recognize quantity is the process of taking in the language of mathematics in its visual form. Speech is the process of putting out language in its oral form.

Recognizing quantity and learning to read numerals are sensory abilities, as is hearing. Talking is a motor ability, as is writing. Talking and writing require motor skills that the baby doesn't have.

The fact that your child is too young to speak and is not able to say his math cards does not negate the fact that you are increasing and enriching his language by teaching him mathematics.

Indeed such investments in teaching the baby will *speed* his talking and broaden his vocabulary. Remember that language is language, whether transmitted to the brain via the eye or via the ear.

Reading his dot cards aloud for a four-month-old is impossible. This is to his great advantage since no one will be tempted to try to get him to do this. He can therefore "read" his dot cards silently, quickly, and effectively.

At this age a tiny child is truly a glutton for information. He will probably demand more information than you are able to give him. When you begin your math program you may often find that at the end of a session he will demand more. Resist the temptation to repeat his cards or do another group just then. He might happily see even more than the two sets of dot cards that you are showing him daily and still want more.

You can actually show several sets back-to-back with a three- or four-month-old and get away with it for a few months but be prepared to change in the near future because you will need to do so.

Remember he is a linguistic genius—be prepared to feed him with a lot of new information.

Starting with a Little Baby (Seven to Twelve Months)

If you are beginning with a seven- to twelve-month-old, the two most important things to keep in mind are:

1. Keep every session *very* brief.
2. Have sessions often.

A four-month-old will sometimes want to see both of his sets of dot cards one after the other at one session. However such a procedure would be a disaster for a seven- to twelve-month-old.

Use only one group of dot cards at a session and then put them away.

The reason for this is simple. Each day your baby's mobility will be expanding. At three months he is relatively sedentary. He is a watcher. He will watch his cards for long periods. We adults love this, so we get into the habit of showing him *all* his cards at one sitting. We get used to this routine; it is easy for us. But each day this baby is changing. He is getting more and more mobile. As soon as he is creeping on hands and knees a whole world of new possibilities opens up for him. He now has a driver's license and he is just dying to explore. All of a sudden this sedentary little fellow, who saw fifty cards quite happily, is no longer sedentary. He has no time at all for his math. We become discouraged. Where have we gone wrong? He must not like mathematics anymore. Baffled, we give up.

The baby must be baffled too. He was having such a good time learning math and then the dot cards and equations disappeared. It wasn't that he stopped liking math, it was that his schedule became busier. He now had an entire household to explore. He has all those kitchen cabinets to open and close, all those plugs to investigate, every piece of fuzz on the carpet has to be picked up and eaten before the sun sets. You have to admit that there is an awful lot on a seven-month-old's plate when it comes to search and destroy. He still wants to explore mathematics too but he cannot afford fifty cards at one time. Five cards at one time is far, far better.

If we provide him with brief sessions, he will continue to gobble up new information at a mile a minute. It is only when we make him late to his next pressing appointment by taking more than a few seconds that he is forced to abandon ship and leave us sitting alone in the middle of the living room floor.

We adults love to find a nice comfortable schedule and then stick to it no matter what. Children are dynamic, they never stop changing. Just as we have established a routine, the tiny child moves on to a new level and we find we must move with him or be left behind.

Because this is so, always keep sessions brief; then as his mobility expands you will be in the habit of brief sessions, which are a natural part of his busy schedule and fit in with his agenda.

Starting with a Baby (Twelve Months to Eighteen Months)

If you are beginning your math program with a child of this age the two most important things to remember are:

1. Very, very brief sessions.
2. Stop before he wants to stop.

In terms of the Math Pathway you will be emphasizing the *first* and *second* and *the third steps* (Chapter Seven). As you work your way up the Math Pathway with a child at this particular stage of development, the most important refinement is to keep the duration of every session *very, very* brief.

The reason this is so important is that now his mobility development becomes extremely important.

At twelve months, a baby is either walking or beginning the process of moving between people or furniture while holding on with his hands in order to work his way by degrees to his first independent steps. By the time that same child is eighteen months old he will not only have become a good steady walker but he will have begun to run. This is quite an accomplishment in six short months. In order to achieve these spectacular results he must put a great deal of time and energy into feats of physical daring.

At no other point in his life will physical movement assume the importance that it does at this moment. You can be assured that if you were to attempt to follow your baby and simply do each of the things he does physically during the day you would be absolutely exhausted after a single hour of his routine. It has been tried.

No adult is physically up to the rigors of what the average twelve- to eighteen-month-old can handle in a given day.

These physical activities are of great importance to the tiny child. During this period of his growth and development we have to be especially wise about adapting his math program to his intense physical program. Up to this moment in his life a group of five dot cards or three equations at one session may be perfect. However, during this stage you may need to drop to three dot cards at a session or two or even one.

There is no single principle of teaching that will take you further than that of always stopping before your child wants to stop.

Always stop before *he* wants to stop.

Always stop *before* he wants to stop.

Always stop before he wants to stop.

This principle is true for all teaching of all human beings at all stages of development and at any age.

But it is *most especially* true for the twelve- to eighteen-month-old.

He needs a high frequency, low duration schedule. Lots of brief sessions suit him. Indeed he needs those brief, treasured respites from his labors.

He will love the entire Math Pathway from the *first step* of recognizing quantities of dots to the *fifth step* of sophisticated equations with numerals, but he will *need extremely short sessions* because he is a man on the move and cannot afford to tarry for very long.

Very short and sweet sessions are best for him.

Starting with a Little Child (Eighteen Months to Thirty Months)

Beginning *anything* new or different with an eighteen- to thirty-month-old can be a challenge. He is of course highly capable and will move through the *first step* to the *fifth step* rapidly *once* we have a happy consistent program *started*. There are two important points to remember when you are teaching this little fellow:

1. Start his math program *gradually.*
2. Move from introducing dot cards to beginning equations as quickly as possible.

As each day passes he develops and he assumes his own viewpoint. He begins to have his own likes and dislikes. The eighteen-month-old is not the pure intellectual he was at three months.

If we are going to begin to introduce language in visual form to an eighteen-month-old we first must remember that he is already an expert at language auditorially. Although he has been talking for months, it is only now that the adults around him can understand his sounds as words. It is not surprising that when he realizes he is at last being understood he has a lot to say and a number of demands to make.

It is important to keep in mind that if an idea is *his* idea it's a great idea; if an idea originates elsewhere it may not have his approval.

No one occupies center stage quite as completely and confidently as this fellow. This is his glory and his program needs to be designed with this in mind.

The first thing to remember is that you cannot go from no math program to a full-blown math program in a single day with this little guy.

Instead of beginning with two sets of five dot cards as outlined in Chapter Seven, begin with only one group of five dot cards. This will pique his interest without going overboard. You need to woo him a little.

He will love math once he decides it is *his idea* and they are *his dot cards* but at first they are your cards and he doesn't know them.

Show him that one group of five dot cards very quickly and then put them away. Come back at another good moment later. In a few days add the second group of five dot cards. When you begin equations by *evolution* as his interest grows, introduce a new set of three equations as the days go on.

It is best to starve him a little and have him pressuring you for more. As your program progresses, ask him what equations he would like and do those with him.

As soon as you have retired dot cards one through twenty, begin equations with him. He will love equations, so don't wait until you have done one to fifty in the dots to get to equations. He is not a baby. He will want equations more than single dot cards, so get to them as quickly as you can.

He will be delighted to major in the *third step* on the Math Pathway and beyond as long as we begin that very *first step* by evolution rather than revolution.

A word about your eighteen to thirty-month-old saying the dots or equations aloud. A child of two, as everyone knows, does exactly and precisely what pleases him most. If he wishes to shout out his equations, he may do so. If he doesn't wish to say them, he won't. The point is to teach your child whatever his age may be and recognize his right to demonstrate his knowledge in the way *he* chooses— or—not at all.

About the Older Child (Thirty Months or Older)

The ability to recognize *real value* or quantity is definitely strongest between the ages of birth and thirty months. The dot cards really are a baby's domain. This does not mean that a child older than thirty months does not have any chance of learning the quantity cards but it does mean that the chances of his doing so are much less.

If your child is only a little bit over this age then you should definitely give the quantity cards a try. You have absolutely nothing to lose and everything to gain if he does well.

If your child is well over thirty months, we recommend doing the quantity cards from one to twenty. If, by good fortune, your child is able to recognize them at this older age that will be wonderful.

If, on the other hand, he cannot, the dot cards from one to twenty will give him a better improved sense of real quantity than he would otherwise have had. This will be to his advantage as he is learning mathematics in the future.

The ability to instantly discern the difference beween 98 dots and 99 dots is a wonderful and wonderous ability. However it is not *everything*. The entire world of higher mathematics is still available to the student even if they are not able to do dots or math equations instantly.

This book is about the very first steps of the enormous language of mathematics. The first step *is* quantity. Unfortunately for you and me, this was a skipped step. This is the step that makes the field of arithmetic easy.

But, in truth, arithmetic is only the beginning. Sadly most adults were taught so badly that they never really got beyond arithmetic. By the time the real fun began, in higher math, you and I had long since given up on the entire subject of mathematics. But what is more important, we gave up on ourselves and our own tremendous ability to understand the language of mathematics and to use it.

Your three-, four-, or five-year-old should not suffer the same fate. There is no reason for it. If he is too old for the dot cards, then by all means go ahead and begin to teach him numerals. You may have to move a bit more slowly and you will definitely have to approach the teaching of equations in a more conventional vein, but remember his ability to take in raw facts will never be better than it is right now.

We have many superb young ten-, eleven- and twelve-year-old mathematicians who are enjoying trigonometry, and they did not begin their home math programs until they were four or five years old and well beyond the age of doing the quantity cards.

Don't become so in love with the notion of instant arithmetic that you miss the forest for the trees.

The objective is a child who embraces the entire realm of the language of mathematics. The beauty and pleasure of this badly neglected science lies in the opportunity to think and reason logically and creatively. One can still appreciate this beauty and experience this pleasure armed with a calculator if necessary.

So don't give up on your older kids—they are mathematicians waiting to be taught also. Get them started as young as possible. You will be surprised at their abilities.

SUMMARY

Once you have begun to teach your child mathematics, one or two things will no doubt occur:

1. You will find everything is going superbly and you are more and more enthusiastic about learning more about how to teach your baby, or—

2. You may have questions or problems.

Trouble Shooting

If you have a question or have run into a problem you cannot solve, do the following:

1. Reread chapters Seven and Eight carefully. The vast majority of all technical questions about mathematics are actually covered in these two chapters. You will spot what you missed the first time and be able to correct it easily. If not, go on to step 2.

2. Reread this book carefully. The vast majority of all philosophical questions about mathematics are covered here. Each time you read the book you will understand it at a higher level since your experience in teaching your child will grow. You will find the answer you need; if not, go on to step 3.

3. Good teachers need a good amount of sleep. Get more sleep. Mothers, especially mothers of very young children, almost never have an adequate amount of sleep. Evaluate honestly how much sleep you get regularly. Add at least an extra hour. If this does not solve the problem, go on to step 4.

4. Get the HOW TO TEACH YOUR BABY MATH Video available from The Gentle Revolution Press. This will enable you to actually see demonstrations of mothers teaching their young children math. Many mothers find this helpful. This will give you the confidence you need. If not, go on to step 5.

5. Write to us and tell us what you are doing and what your question is. We personally answer every letter and have done so for more than a quarter of a century. It may take us time to get back to you because mothers write to us from all over the world, so be certain you have *really* explored steps one through four first. But, if all else fails, please write.

More Information

If you want to learn more about how to teach your baby, do the following:

1. Attend the How to Multiply Your Baby's Intelligence course presented by the Institutes for the Achievement of Human Potential in Philadelphia. This is a seven-day course for mothers and fathers. Mathematics is only one of the many subjects that are covered. This is a wonderful course that every mother or father should attend while their children are still young or when parents are expecting a new baby.

2. Read the other books in the *Gentle Revolution Series* listed in the back of this book.

3. Get the materials available in the *Gentle Revolution Series* listed in the back of this book.

4. Write to us at the Institutes and tell us what you are doing and how your child is progressing. Your information is precious to us and invaluable to future generations of mothers.

13

On Respect

Learning is one of the greatest joys in life and it should remain so. Remember you are building into your child a love of learning that will multiply throughout his life. More accurately, you are reinforcing a built-in rage to learn which will not be denied but which can certainly be twisted into useless or even negative channels. Play the game joyously.

You are giving your child an unparalleled opportunity for knowledge by opening the golden door to all the fascinating problems that can be solved by mathematics.

Bear in mind that numerals, at which we adults are trained, are abstract and without meaning except as symbols to represent numbers. Actual numbers on the other hand, at which children are superb, are as concrete as it's possible to be. So concrete that the child can actually "see" the number in his mind's eye and can "read" the actual number as we can read only the numeral. That's why the tiny kid can answer the math problem almost the instant you present it.

He's a great deal like those annoying little calculators. We say to our tiny calculator by pushing its buttons, "Calculator, what is 987 multiplied by 654?"

We push the equal button and, faster than the eye can see, the answer appears—645,498. That's insulting in the extreme. Here is four dollars' worth of plastic and wires answering with the push of a button and without hesitation a problem that we human beings with our vast and incredible human cortex can answer only after much written calculation. Yet we human beings master English, French, or German without the slightest effort when we are children. No computer in the world, no matter how complex, no matter what its multimillion dollar cost, can carry on a true free-wheeling conversation with another computer. It's the paradox to end all paradoxes. It is, in short, an absurdity. Happily, the tiny child is capable of upholding the honor of the human brain. He, like the four dollar's worth of plastic and wire, is always looking at the answer and knows it instantly. There are in the world a handful of adult mathematical geniuses who can do the same. There is a Dutch mathematician at the CERN (European Center for Nuclear Research), a man named Willem Klein, who can in two minutes and forty-three seconds solve totally, in his head, the 73rd root of a 499 digit numeral. An electronic computer confirmed the human solution—6,789,235.

In this respect he is like the tiny children.

Who is surprised that he understood math as a tiny child? He does not find it necessary to play the dumb old "carry the 7" rituals by which we were taught to do math and were thus condemned to a lifetime of painfully complicated (and as a result frequently inaccurate) recipes. It should be mentioned that the author, being already grown-up, is as condemned to the old methods as the reader is likely to be.

Remember that children are learning every waking minute, and we are teaching them all the time, but the problem is that we are not always aware that we are teaching them and thus we may be teaching them something we do not intend to teach them.

Go very quickly or you will make him frantic with boredom. Recently one of our mothers, who was teaching her daughter the dot cards, was going very slowly (because she was afraid that her daughter didn't truly understand the dots) and was very quietly, but very effectively, reprimanded by her three-year-old.

This tiny child in exasperation said, "Oh, Mother!", took the dot cards, and selected several of them. Marching into the dining room, she put the card with thirty-two dots on her father's plate, the card with thirty dots on her mother's plate, the card with eight dots on her brother's plate, the card with five dots on her sister's plate, and the card with three dots on her own plate. It took her mother a while to figure out that she had placed each person's age in dots on his or her plate. Children who know math ask all sorts of questions about numbers and remember the answers. Her mother got the message and moved five times faster.

Remember that tiny kids don't know that we adults can't do it.

One of our wise grandmothers held up a card with sixty-nine dots and asked her three-year-old granddaughter a dumb question.

"How many dots can you see, dear?"

"Why, all of them, Grandmother."

Ask a dumb question and you'll get a smart answer.

Historically, we have not only dreadfully underestimated the tiny child's ability to do math (while substantially overestimating our own ability) but we have given him material to work with that falls far short of his ability and his level of enjoyment. It is a miracle we have not bored him to death, instead of just boring him to the point of not wanting to do math.

We give five-year-olds problems to solve that would bore a two-year-old to tears. Can you imagine two-year-olds who can do equations in nothing flat faced with a book that explains that two fuzzy bears who meet three fuzzy bears are all together five fuzzy bears?

The idea that tiny children are dehydrated adults who must deal with dehydrated numbers is most certainly a silly one.

Tiny kids can learn anything that you can present to them in an honest and factual way. If you give them the facts they'll deduce the laws that govern them. That is exactly the same method that scientists use to discover laws.

So, don't give them theories and abstractions, give them facts, give them reality. From the facts little children are brilliantly able to intuit the laws.

The dictionary defines science as "that branch of knowledge that deals with a body of facts systematically arranged to reveal the laws that govern them."

According to this definition, tiny kids *are* scientists.

You are now an expert teacher. You have taught a small child to do math, something very few people have done. The world of numbers is now his oyster. Using whatever method you think wise, teach him everything you like. Buy him a small but real calculator after he's off and running. He'll astonish you with what he learns, and the sky's the limit. All the general rules we have proposed still apply.

Bring great excitement to the game each time you play it. The tiny child has an incredible ability to take in facts but he will take all his cues from you in determining what is of real value and what isn't.

Do not push him.

Do not bore him. In all cases stop before he wants to stop. Do not persist in your teaching for more than a few minutes at a time, but do it often.

Always remember that math is a game. It is fun! It is playing with your baby. In our experience those mothers who approached the teaching of math with casual gaiety and imagination and who shouted their enthusiasm at each new accomplishment with unalloyed happiness, succeeded better than those mothers who showed intellectual objectivity and sober praise. Remember that you are not the Secretary of Education. You're his mother and you're on his side. Teaching is not a chore; it must not be a grind.

Once your child's free and running, you will have a thinker on your hands and there will be no stopping him. It seems a little silly to say at this point that math, like reading, is basic to all education, to virtually all learning in the world we know. You will have opened the doors to learning, the greatest treasury that life has to offer except, perhaps, love and respect (that is, emotional response and responsibility), without which nothing is really worthwhile.

In the process of teaching your baby math, both of you will have learned more about love and respect.

The gentle revolution has begun. Thus far it has been an exhilarating journey in which our mothers have discovered an even greater love and a deeper respect for their babies than they had imagined possible. They have also discovered within themselves a wellspring of enthusiasm for teaching their babies and enjoying the fruits of a second education more subtle and more profound than the first.

Now that the secret is out, it is no longer a question of whether little kids can do math—it's a question of how far they'll take it. The new question will be, we guess—when hundreds of thousands of preschool kids can do math and thus increase the world's knowledge beyond anybody's wildest dreams—what will they do with this old world?

If indeed knowledge leads to good, surely this world will be a better place when its children are more capable and as a consequence more confident of their own superb abilities and more able to use those abilities to solve the problems that beset us.

This, after all, is what the gentle revolution is all about.

Acknowledgements

The basic ideas that this book contains are so simple and obvious that it is difficult to believe that someone, or lots of people, haven't seen them before. So far as we have been able to determine, no one has. Or at least no one has ever expounded them clearly enough to be understood or perhaps strongly enough to be heard.

If, in fact, someone else has expounded them but has not been heard, I strongly suspect that it was because he or she was alone.

Nobody ever wrote a book by himself.

Especially this one.

If *we* are heard it will be because of the following people:

Janet Doman, my daughter, Director of the Institutes for the Achievement of Human Potential and Suzy Aisen, Director of the Institutes for the Achievement of Intellectual Excellence. They developed the methods of instruction and did the teaching. They were virtually co-authors.

Gretchen Kerr, the former director of the Institutes, who so ably took over my duties while she sent me away to write this book.

Katie Doman, my wife, who first taught mothers how to teach their babies to read, to do math and to multiply their intelligence and who still does it superbly.

Donald Barnhouse, an experienced math teacher who serves as a consultant to the Evan Thomas Institute and who made several helpful additions and corrections to this revised edition of the book.

Greta Erdtmann, my research assistant, and Cathy Ruhling, Director of Communications, who conferred loving care upon the manuscript through the dead of night and upon me as well.

Michael Armentrout, Director for Special Projects, who conferred the same loving care on the manuscript of the revised edition that had been bestowed on the original edition.

Our parents of brain-injured kids who through their creativity and endless determination helped to forge the math pathway.

The incredible mothers and tiny children of the Evan Thomas Institute who followed and helped to perfect that pathway.

The senior staff of the Institutes for the Achievement of Intellectual Excellence: Miki Nakayachi, Phyllis Kimmel, Teruki Uemura, Janet Caputo, Carol Newell, Charlotte Law, James Kaliss, Kathy Myers, Janet Gauger, Anita Barnes, Christine Tagert, Barbara Dadourian.

Douglas Doman, my son, Vice Director of the Institutes for the Achievement of Human Potential.

Roselise Wilkinson, M.D., Medical Director of the Institutes for the Achievement of Human Potential.

Elaine Lee, Director of Children's Affairs at the Institutes.

Mathew Newell, Director of the Institutes for the Achievement of Physical Excellence; Rosalind Doman, my daughter-in-law, associate director; Rumiko Ion, vice director; and the senior staff: Marlene Marckwordt, and Miki Mock.

Ann Ball, Director of the Institutes for the Achievement of Physiological Excellence; and the senior staff: Dawn Price and Ernesto Vasquez, M.D.

Robert Derr, the Administrator of the Institutes.

Neil Harvey, Ph.D., Director of the Temple Fay Institute for Academics.

The International Board of Directors of the Institutes for the Achievement of Human Potential: Pio Bonvincini, Michael Burke, Joseph Gay, Harry Guenther, Nigel Hawthorne, Sherman Hines, Kaname Matsuzawa, Liza Minnelli, Robert Morris, William Mueller, Richard Norton, Ralph Pelligra,

M.D., Philip Phillips, Jonathan Slevin, Jose Carlos Veras, Chatham R. Wheat III and John Wright.

Neither this book nor any other books the staff have written would have been possible without the constant and generous support of the following people:

The hundreds of thousands of members of the United Steel Workers of America.

NASA, Ames
The Friends of the Institutes.
The Sony Corporation
John and Mary McShain
Liza Minnelli
Jerry and Maureen Morantz
Walter G. Buckner
John and Josie Connelly
Sam and Joan Metzger
Dan and Margaret Melcher
Masaru and Yoshiko Ibuka
Louise Sacchi

Finally, I wish to bow to all those in history who have believed with a consuming passion that children were really quite superior to the image that we adults have always held of them.

About the Authors

Glenn Doman received his degree in physical therapy from the University of Pennsylvania in 1940. From that point on, he began pioneering the field of child brain development. In 1955, he founded The Institutes for the Achievement of Human Potential in Philadelphia. By the early sixties, the world-renowned work of The Institutes with brain-injured children had led to vital discoveries about the growth and development of well children. The author has lived with, studied and worked with children in more than 100 nations, ranging from the most civilized to the most primitive. The Brazilian government knighted him for his outstanding work on behalf of the children of the world.

Glenn Doman is the international best-selling author of the Gentle Revolution Series, consisting of *How to Teach Your Baby to Read, How to Teach Your Baby Math, How to Multiply Your Baby's Intelligence, How to Give Your Baby Encyclopedic Knowledge*, and *How to Teach Your Baby to Be Physically Superb*. He is also the author of *What to Do About Your Brain-Injured Child*, a guide for parents of hurt children. Currently, he continues to devote all of his time teaching parents of both hurt and well children.

For more than thirty years Glenn Doman and the child brain developmentalists of The Institutes have been demonstrating that very young children are far more capable of learning than we ever imagined. He has taken this remarkable work—work that explores why children from birth to age six learn better and faster than older children do—and given it practical application. As the founder of The Institutes for the Achievement of Human Potential, he has created a comprehensive early development program that any parent can follow at home.

When Glenn Doman decided to update the books of the Gentle Revolution Series it was only natural that his daughter help him to edit and organize the additional information gained over the last three decades of experience since some of the books were originally written.

Janet Doman is the director of the Institutes for the Achievement of Human Potential. After completing studies in zoology at the University of Hull in England and physical anthropology at the University of Pennsylvania, she devoted herself to teaching early reading programs to parents at The Institutes. She spent almost two years at the Early Development Association in Japan where she created programs for mothers. From there she returned to Philadelphia to direct the Evan Thomas Institute, a unique school for mothers and babies. The early development program led to the creation of the International School for the children who graduated from the early development program.

Janet spends most of her day nose-to-nose with "the best mothers in the world," helping them to discover the vast potential of their babies and their own potential as teachers.

Appendix

Equations and Number Personalities

by Donald Barnhouse

Every number has its own character. Some who love math might even say "personality." But to say that numbers have character is no exaggeration at all. Zero and one are the superstars. Speaking only about the numbers represented on the Dot Cards, ten and one hundred are very special in today's world, because the decimal (ten-based) numeration system is so completely woven into our culture. Two, four, eight, and all the other powers of two are very special; they are building blocks of the binary (two-based) numeration system that computers use heavily. Mechanical counters on everything from cars to copy machines start at zero, go up to nine, and then turn to zero again. But we do not measure a child's height up to three feet nine inches and then go to four feet; we group inches by twelves. Clocks do the same with hours. The newborn's weight is not measured up to six pounds nine ounces and then rolled over to seven pounds; we group ounces (and some computer bits) by sixteens. It takes babies a while to learn all this, but the numbers themselves are universal, and even tiny children perceive them immediately.

One great virtue of the Dot Cards is that the number of dots on the card does not depend on the numeration system. A Roman child of a thousand years ago, a Hindu child of two thousand years ago, and an Egyptian child of three thousand years ago would see exactly the same number of dots on any Dot Card as your child will see. But as soon as we give a name to that number, we mark ourselves as belonging to a certain culture. The showing of the Dot Cards is tied to the ten-based numeration system used in most of the world.

As soon as you pick up a card and say to your child "Seventy-four!" you have identified yourself as belonging to a culture which groups that collection of red circles into seven groups of ten and four single dots. In a hexagesimal world, you would have called out "Four-A!" When you say "Seventy-four!" you are saying, in effect, "seven tens and four ones." Your child will have absorbed at least part of the significance of this by the time you have shown the cards the appropriate number of times. He will certainly have noticed the similarity of the names that end in "-teen," and the abrupt change to twenty. He will have noticed the similar sounding endings to all the multiples of ten from then on: thir*ty*, for*ty*, fif*ty*, and so on. He will have made a connection between the sounds "seven" and "seventeen" and "seventy." He will surely have heard the names of the first nine cards repeated over and over. He will have noticed that every time a card is shown with one more dot than on the cards whose names end in "-ty," he hears "-one." We may not know exactly how he has processed all that information and what he does with it, but it is certainly in there.

The French child will have points of additional interest, or confusion, depending on how you look at it, for after their word for sixty they have no words corresponding to the later multiples of ten. What we call seventy they call sixty-ten; seventy-nine for them is sixty-nineteen; eighty for them is four-twenty; ninety is four-twenty-ten; and ninety-seven is four-twenty-seventeen.

All these facts and more play into the choice of the equations we have listed on the back of the Dot Cards for use when you are ready for that stage. The numbers with lots of character have more equations than those with less. Some are so interesting, like 60 and 30, that there is not nearly room enough for all the fascinating relationships we could have expressed through equations. Others are so boring (Forgive me, 83 and 91!) that it is hard to find anything at all interesting to say about them.

This is the **general** plan. In one corner of each card you will usually find an attempt at basic identification of each number (how many tens and how many ones), and at locating it in the order of numbers. In another you will find a look at its factors (what numbers can be multiplied together to get it), and the more factors a number has, generally speaking, the more interesting it is. The third corner may show interesting sequences that add up to the number, if there are any. In the fourth corner are some key subtractions that yield the number. Other relationships, including some that will help with later learning of addition facts and multiplication facts, are scattered where there is room.

It is not possible in a brief space to indicate all the reasons for all the equations, but a serious attempt has been made to relate them to further mathematical learning. There are other facts implicit in the choice of equations that may escape you, but your child may well pick them up. For example, if it were not mentioned here, you might not notice that every card where you find an equation showing the sum of three consecutive numbers is a number divisible by three. Your child will notice and think about that. He will also notice a group of cards with equations showing the number equal to the sum of four consecutive numbers. Can you figure out which numbers can be expressed that way? Do not doubt that your child will work at it; children less than eighteen hours old have been proved beyond any doubt to be interested in, and capable of, analytical reasoning.

In sum, the nature of the equations is intended to communicate subliminally, as well as directly, something of the essential mystique of what mathematics is, and what its place in the broader realm of knowledge is. Pythagoras was not far wrong when his insights into math and music, and his perception of the relations between them, prompted him to share his enthusiasms in such a way that some of his students appear to have made a kind of religion out of it.

One point which the choice of equations is intended to communicate (beyond the simple math facts in them) is that mathematics is the opposite of chaos. Mathematics is order. Mathematics is one of our primary tools for turning chaos into order. The great American poet Mark VanDoren wrote a sonnet which includes this couplet:

There are no lines in nature, false or true,
Till number cuts a door, and pulls it to.

Obviously there is an infinite number of equations one could write for each number. We have not selected a simple random sample of those which are true. Those which appear to have no rhyme or reason behind them have been avoided. We have felt it would be wasting precious space on the back of the 60 card with an equation like $42 + 37 - 54 + 23 - 7 + 19 = 60$. And it would be meaningless to put $42 + 37 - 54 + 23 - 6 + 19 = 61$ on the back of the 61 card, though it is true. Only accountants will ever in their lives see numbers in unrelated ways, and we can be grateful that computers have almost completely freed people from dealing with such equations. Such equations are like magicians' patter, chaos and confusion which obscure what is really significant. Math offers a vision of the beauty and character as well as the function of numbers. It is our hope that the combination of Dot Cards and equations can introduce arithmetic far more realistically and far more interestingly that it usually appears to school children.

Examples of Equations
for the backs of dot cards 0 to 60

0

$1 \times 0 = 0$

$2 \times 0 = 0$

$3 \times 0 = 0$

$5 \times 0 = 0$

$11 \times 0 = 0$

$59 \times 0 = 0$

$1 - 1 = 0$

$2 - 2 = 0$

$3 - 3 = 0$

$8 - 8 = 0$

$47 - 47 = 0$

$65 - 65 = 0$

$0 + 0 = 0$

$0 - 0 = 0$

$0 \times 0 = 0$

$0 \div 2 = 0$

$0 \div 9 = 0$

$0 \div 73 = 0$

$4 \times 5 \times 0 = 0$

$20 \div 2 \times 0 = 0$

$6 \times 0 \times 8 \times 5 = 0$

$24 \div 3 \times 0 = 0$

$14 \times 0 \div 7 = 0$

$100 \times 0 \div 10 = 0$

1

$1 \times 1 = 1$

$1 \times 1 \times 1 \times$
$1 \times 1 = 1$

$0 + 1 = 1$

$1 \div 1 = 1$

$1 \times 1 \div 1 \div$
$1 \times 1 = 1$

$11 - 10 = 1$

$21 - 20 = 1$

$31 - 30 = 1$

$2 - 1 = 1$

$100 - 99 = 1$

$2 \times 2 \div 4 = 1$

$3 \times 2 \div 6 = 1$

$5 \times 3 \div 15 = 1$

$7 \times 5 \div 35 = 1$

$1 \times 2 \times 3 \times$
$4 \div 24 = 1$

$7 \div 7 = 1$

$18 \div 18 = 1$

$23 \div 23 = 1$

$41 \div 41 = 1$

$65 \div 65 = 1$

2

$$0 + 2 = 2$$
$$2 + 0 = 2$$
$$1 + 1 = 2$$
$$2 \times 1 = 2$$
$$2 \div 1 = 2$$

$$12 - 10 = 2$$
$$22 - 20 = 2$$
$$32 - 30 = 2$$
$$72 - 70 = 2$$
$$100 - 98 = 2$$

$$3 - 1 = 2$$
$$4 - 2 = 2$$
$$5 - 3 = 2$$
$$6 - 4 = 2$$
$$7 - 5 = 2$$

$$4 \div 2 = 2$$
$$6 \div 3 = 2$$
$$8 \div 4 = 2$$
$$10 \div 5 = 2$$
$$20 \div 10 = 2$$

3

$$3 + 0 = 3$$
$$2 + 1 = 3$$
$$1 + 1 + 1 = 3$$
$$3 \times 1 = 3$$
$$1 \times 3 = 3$$

$$13 - 10 = 3$$
$$43 - 40 = 3$$
$$10 - 7 = 3$$
$$9 - 6 = 3$$
$$8 - 5 = 3$$

$$6 \times 5 \div 10 = 3$$
$$9 \times 10 \div 30 = 3$$
$$4 \times 15 \div 20 = 3$$
$$12 \times 2 \div 8 = 3$$
$$3 \times 24 \div 24 = 3$$

$$6 \div 2 = 3$$
$$9 \div 3 = 3$$
$$12 \div 4 = 3$$
$$15 \div 5 = 3$$
$$30 \div 10 = 3$$

4

$0 + 4 = 4$
$1 + 3 = 4$
$2 + 2 = 4$
$1 \times 4 = 4$
$2 \times 2 = 4$

$9 - 5 = 4$
$8 - 4 = 4$
$7 - 3 = 4$
$6 - 2 = 4$
$5 - 1 = 4$

$14 - 10 = 4$
$34 - 30 = 4$
$74 - 70 = 4$
$100 - 96 = 4$
$10 - 6 = 4$

$4 \div 1 = 4$
$8 \div 2 = 4$
$12 \div 3 = 4$
$40 \div 10 = 4$
$100 \div 25 = 4$

5

$0 + 5 = 5$
$1 + 4 = 5$
$2 + 3 = 5$
$5 \times 1 = 5$
$5 \div 1 = 5$

$15 - 10 = 5$
$45 - 40 = 5$
$85 - 80 = 5$
$100 - 95 = 5$
$10 - 5 = 5$

$9 - 4 = 5$
$8 - 3 = 5$
$7 - 2 = 5$
$6 - 1 = 5$
$5 - 0 = 5$

$10 \div 2 = 5$
$15 \div 3 = 5$
$20 \div 4 = 5$
$50 \div 10 = 5$
$100 \div 20 = 5$

6

0 + 6 = 6	16 − 10 = 6
1 + 5 = 6	46 − 40 = 6
2 + 4 = 6	96 − 90 = 6
3 + 3 = 6	100 − 94 = 6
1 + 2 + 3 = 6	10 − 4 = 6
1 × 2 × 3 = 6	9 − 3 = 6

4 × 12 ÷ 8 = 6	12 ÷ 2 = 6
2 × 18 ÷ 6 = 6	18 ÷ 3 = 6
3 × 10 ÷ 5 = 6	24 ÷ 4 = 6
8 × 3 ÷ 4 = 6	30 ÷ 5 = 6
45 × 2 ÷ 15 = 6	60 ÷ 10 = 6
24 × 3 ÷ 12 = 6	90 ÷ 15 = 6

7

6 + 1 = 7	17 − 10 = 7
5 + 2 = 7	37 − 30 = 7
4 + 3 = 7	100 − 93 = 7
7 × 1 = 7	10 − 3 = 7

14 − 7 = 7	14 ÷ 2 = 7
21 − 14 = 7	21 ÷ 3 = 7
28 − 21 = 7	28 ÷ 4 = 7
35 − 28 = 7	35 ÷ 5 = 7

8

$$7 + 1 = 8$$
$$6 + 2 = 8$$
$$5 + 3 = 8$$
$$4 + 4 = 8$$
$$2 \times 4 = 8$$
$$2 \times 2 \times 2 = 8$$

$$18 - 10 = 8$$
$$28 - 20 = 8$$
$$98 - 90 = 8$$
$$100 - 92 = 8$$
$$10 - 2 = 8$$
$$9 - 1 = 8$$

$$4 \times 4 \div 2 = 8$$
$$4 \times 4 \times 4 \div 8 = 8$$
$$5 \times 16 \div 10 = 8$$
$$24 \times 3 \div 9 = 8$$
$$10 \times 4 \div 5 = 8$$
$$16 \times 2 \div 4 = 8$$

$$8 \div 1 = 8$$
$$16 \div 2 = 8$$
$$24 \div 3 = 8$$
$$32 \div 4 = 8$$
$$40 \div 5 = 8$$
$$88 \div 11 = 8$$

9

$$8 + 1 = 9$$
$$7 + 2 = 9$$
$$6 + 3 = 9$$
$$5 + 4 = 9$$
$$3 \times 3 = 9$$

$$81 \div 9 = 9$$
$$72 \div 8 = 9$$
$$63 \div 7 = 9$$
$$54 \div 6 = 9$$
$$9 \div 1 = 9$$

$$3 + 3 + 3 = 9$$
$$2 + 3 + 4 = 9$$
$$1 + 3 + 5 = 9$$
$$100 - 91 = 9$$
$$10 - 1 = 9$$

$$18 \div 2 = 9$$
$$27 \div 3 = 9$$
$$36 \div 4 = 9$$
$$45 \div 5 = 9$$
$$19 - 10 = 9$$

204

10

$$1 + 9 = 10$$
$$2 + 8 = 10$$
$$3 + 7 = 10$$
$$4 + 6 = 10$$
$$5 + 5 = 10$$

$$20 \div 2 = 10$$
$$30 \div 3 = 10$$
$$40 \div 4 = 10$$
$$70 \div 7 = 10$$
$$100 \div 10 = 10$$

$$1 + 2 + 3 + 4 = 10$$
$$20 - 10 = 10$$
$$30 - 20 = 10$$
$$80 - 70 = 10$$
$$100 - 90 = 10$$

$$19 - 9 = 10$$
$$18 - 8 = 10$$
$$17 - 7 = 10$$
$$16 - 6 = 10$$
$$15 - 5 = 10$$

11

$$10 + 1 = 11$$
$$9 + 2 = 11$$
$$8 + 3 = 11$$
$$7 + 4 = 11$$
$$6 + 5 = 11$$

$$99 \div 9 = 11$$
$$88 \div 8 = 11$$
$$77 \div 7 = 11$$
$$33 \div 3 = 11$$
$$22 \div 2 = 11$$

$$20 - 9 = 11$$
$$100 - 89 = 11$$
$$11 + 0 = 11$$
$$11 - 0 = 11$$
$$11 \div 1 = 11$$

$$22 - 11 = 11$$
$$33 - 22 = 11$$
$$44 - 33 = 11$$
$$55 - 44 = 11$$
$$66 - 55 = 11$$

204

12

11 + 1 = 12	2 × 6 = 12
10 + 2 = 12	2 × 2 × 3 = 12
9 + 3 = 12	4 × 3 = 12
8 + 4 = 12	3 + 3 + 3 + 3 = 12
7 + 5 = 12	4 + 4 + 4 = 12
6 + 6 = 12	3 + 4 + 5 = 12

6 × 4 ÷ 2 = 12	24 ÷ 2 = 12
4 × 9 ÷ 3 = 12	36 ÷ 3 = 12
15 × 4 ÷ 5 = 12	48 ÷ 4 = 12
3 × 24 ÷ 6 = 12	60 ÷ 5 = 12
16 × 6 ÷ 8 = 12	100 − 88 = 12
3 × 4 ÷ 1 = 12	20 − 8 = 12

13

10 + 3 = 13	9 + 4 = 13
12 + 1 = 13	8 + 5 = 13
13 × 1 = 13	7 + 6 = 13

52 − 39 = 13	52 ÷ 4 = 13
39 − 26 = 13	26 ÷ 2 = 13
26 − 13 = 13	39 ÷ 3 = 13

14

$$10 + 4 = 14$$
$$13 + 1 = 14$$
$$14 + 0 = 14$$

$$9 + 5 = 14$$
$$8 + 6 = 14$$
$$7 + 7 = 14$$

$$2 + 3 +$$
$$4 + 5 = 14$$
$$100 - 86 = 14$$
$$20 - 6 = 14$$

$$2 \times 7 = 14$$
$$7 \times 2 = 14$$
$$14 \times 1 = 14$$

15

$$10 + 5 = 15$$
$$14 + 1 = 15$$
$$3 \times 5 = 15$$
$$5 + 5 + 5 = 15$$
$$4 + 5 + 6 = 15$$

$$7 + 8 = 15$$
$$6 + 9 = 15$$
$$1 + 2 + 3 +$$
$$4 + 5 = 15$$
$$3 + 5 + 7 = 15$$
$$8 + 7 = 15$$

$$100 - 85 = 15$$
$$20 - 5 = 15$$
$$21 - 6 = 15$$
$$22 - 7 = 15$$
$$23 - 8 = 15$$

$$30 \div 2 = 15$$
$$45 \div 3 = 15$$
$$5 \times 12 \div 4 = 15$$
$$3 \times 25 \div 5 = 15$$
$$9 \times 10 \div 6 = 15$$

16

$$10 + 6 = 16$$
$$15 + 1 = 16$$
$$100 - 84 = 16$$
$$20 - 4 = 16$$

$$2 \times 8 = 16$$
$$4 \times 4 = 16$$
$$2 \times 2 \times 2 \times 2 = 16$$
$$8 \times 2 = 16$$

$$9 + 7 = 16$$
$$8 + 8 = 16$$
$$1 + 7 + 3 + 5 = 16$$
$$1 + 3 + 5 + 7 = 16$$

$$32 \div 2 = 16$$
$$48 \div 3 = 16$$
$$64 \div 4 = 16$$
$$80 \div 5 = 16$$

17

$$10 + 7 = 17$$
$$16 + 1 = 17$$
$$9 + 8 = 17$$

$$100 - 83 = 17$$
$$20 - 3 = 17$$
$$17 \times 1 = 17$$

$$21 - 4 = 17$$
$$22 - 5 = 17$$
$$23 - 6 = 17$$

$$24 - 7 = 17$$
$$25 - 8 = 17$$
$$26 - 9 = 17$$

18

10 + 8 = 18	2 × 9 = 18
17 + 1 = 18	3 × 6 = 18
9 + 9 = 18	6 + 6 + 6 = 18
3 + 6 + 4 + 5 = 18	5 + 6 + 7 = 18
3 + 4 + 5 + 6 = 18	4 + 6 + 8 = 18

100 − 82 = 18	24 − 6 = 18
20 − 2 = 18	30 − 12 = 18
21 − 3 = 18	36 − 18 = 18
22 − 4 = 18	36 ÷ 2 = 18
23 − 5 = 18	9 × 6 ÷ 3 = 18

19

10 + 9 = 19	100 − 81 = 19
18 + 1 = 19	20 − 1 = 19
19 × 1 = 19	30 − 11 = 19

21 − 2 = 19	24 − 5 = 19
22 − 3 = 19	25 − 6 = 19
23 − 4 = 19	26 − 7 = 19

20

$19 + 1 = 20$
$10 + 10 = 20$
$2 \times 10 = 20$
$2 \times 2 \times 5 = 20$
$4 \times 5 = 20$

$11 + 9 = 20$
$12 + 8 = 20$
$13 + 7 = 20$
$14 + 6 = 20$
$15 + 5 = 20$

$5 \times 8 \div 2 = 20$
$4 \times 15 \div 3 = 20$
$5 \times 12 \div 3 = 20$
$16 \times 5 \div 4 = 20$
$100 \div 5 = 20$

$5 + 5 + 5 + 5 = 20$
$4 + 4 + 4 + $
$4 + 4 = 20$
$100 - 80 = 20$
$90 - 70 = 20$
$80 - 60 = 20$

21

$20 + 1 = 21$
$15 + 6 = 21$
$1 + 2 + 3 + $
$4 + 5 + 6 = 21$
$6 + 9 + 6 = 21$

$3 \times 7 = 21$
$7 + 7 + 7 = 21$
$6 + 7 + 8 = 21$
$5 + 7 + 9 = 21$

$100 - 79 = 21$
$30 - 9 = 21$
$9 \times 7 \div 3 = 21$
$6 \times 7 \div 2 = 21$

$14 + 7 = 21$
$28 - 7 = 21$
$35 - 14 = 21$
$42 - 21 = 21$

22

$$20 + 2 = 22$$
$$21 + 1 = 22$$
$$66 \div 3 = 22$$

$$2 \times 11 = 22$$
$$11 + 11 = 22$$
$$4 + 5 + 6 + 7 = 22$$

$$13 + 9 = 22$$
$$14 + 8 = 22$$
$$15 + 7 = 22$$

$$77 - 55 = 22$$
$$55 - 33 = 22$$
$$88 - 66 = 22$$

23

$$20 + 3 = 23$$
$$22 + 1 = 23$$
$$23 \times 1 = 23$$

$$14 + 9 = 23$$
$$15 + 8 = 23$$
$$16 + 7 = 23$$

$$19 + 4 = 23$$
$$18 + 5 = 23$$
$$17 + 6 = 23$$

$$100 - 77 = 23$$
$$50 - 27 = 23$$
$$30 - 7 = 23$$

24

$20 + 4 = 24$
$23 + 1 = 24$
$8 + 8 + 8 = 24$
$7 + 8 + 9 = 24$
$6 + 8 + 10 = 24$

$2 \times 12 = 24$
$3 \times 8 = 24$
$4 \times 6 = 24$
$1 \times 2 \times 3 \times 4 = 24$
$2 \times 2 \times 2 \times 3 = 24$

$30 - 6 = 24$
$100 - 76 = 24$
$50 - 26 = 24$
$33 - 9 = 24$
$32 - 8 = 24$

$8 \times 6 \div 2 = 24$
$9 \times 8 \div 3 = 24$
$48 \div 6 \times 3 = 24$
$30 \div 5 \times 4 = 24$
$21 \div 7 \times 8 = 24$

25

$20 + 5 = 25$
$24 + 1 = 25$
$30 - 5 = 25$
$100 - 75 = 25$

$5 \times 5 = 25$
$5 + 5 + 5 + 5 + 5 = 25$
$3 + 4 + 5 + 6 + 7 = 25$
$1 + 3 + 5 + 7 + 9 = 25$

$19 + 6 = 25$
$18 + 7 = 25$
$17 + 8 = 25$
$16 + 9 = 25$

$50 \div 2 = 25$
$75 \div 3 = 25$
$100 \div 4 = 25$
$25 \div 1 = 25$

26

$20 + 6 = 26$
$25 + 1 = 26$
$26 \times 1 = 26$

$100 - 74 = 26$
$50 - 24 = 26$
$30 - 4 = 26$

$52 \div 2 = 26$
$39 - 13 = 26$
$39 + 13 - 26 = 26$

$2 \times 13 = 26$
$5 + 6 + 7 + 8 = 26$
$13 + 13 = 26$

27

$20 + 7 = 27$
$26 + 1 = 27$
$100 - 73 = 27$
$50 - 23 = 27$
$30 - 3 = 27$

$3 \times 9 = 27$
$9 + 9 + 9 = 27$
$10 + 9 + 8 = 27$
$11 + 9 + 7 = 27$
$12 + 9 + 6 = 27$

$36 - 9 = 27$
$35 - 8 = 27$
$34 - 7 = 27$
$33 - 6 = 27$
$32 - 5 = 27$

$3 \times 3 \times 3 = 27$
$18 + 9 = 27$
$45 - 18 = 27$
$54 - 27 = 27$
$63 - 36 = 27$

28

$20 + 8 = 28$
$27 + 1 = 28$
$30 - 2 = 28$
$56 - 28 = 28$

$2 \times 14 = 28$
$4 \times 7 = 28$
$2 \times 2 \times 7 = 28$
$8 \times 7 \div 2 = 28$

$100 - 72 = 28$
$50 - 22 = 28$
$4 + 6 +$
$8 + 10 = 28$
$10 + 4 +$
$8 + 6 = 28$

$1 + 2 + 3 + 4 +$
$5 + 6 + 7 = 28$
$1 + 5 + 9 + 13 = 28$
$1 + 6 + 2 + 5 +$
$3 + 4 + 7 = 28$
$7 + 7 + 7 + 7 = 28$

29

$20 + 9 = 29$
$28 + 1 = 29$
$29 \times 1 = 29$

$100 - 71 = 29$
$50 - 21 = 29$
$30 - 1 = 29$

$31 - 2 = 29$
$32 - 3 = 29$
$33 - 4 = 29$

$34 - 5 = 29$
$35 - 6 = 29$
$36 - 7 = 29$

30

$3 \times 10 = 30$ $2 \times 15 = 30$
$29 + 1 = 30$ $3 \times 10 = 30$
$10 + 10 + 10 = 30$ $5 \times 6 = 30$
$9 + 10 + 11 = 30$ $2 \times 3 \times 5 = 30$
$8 + 10 + 12 = 30$ $60 \div 2 = 30$
$5 + 10 + 15 = 30$ $90 \div 3 = 30$
$5 + 5 + 5 +$ $45 - 15 = 30$
$5 + 5 + 5 = 30$

$21 + 9 = 30$ $6 + 7 + 8 + 9 = 30$
$22 + 8 = 30$ $6 + 9 + 7 + 8 = 30$
$23 + 7 = 30$ $15 + 15 = 30$
$24 + 6 = 30$ $12 + 3 + 9 + 6 = 30$
$25 + 5 = 30$ $3 + 6 + 9 + 12 = 30$
$100 - 70 = 30$ $4 + 5 + 6 + 7 + 8 = 30$
$90 - 60 = 30$ $6 + 6 + 6 + 6 + 6 = 30$

31

$30 + 1 = 31$ $31 \times 1 = 31$
$21 + 10 = 31$ $32 - 1 = 31$
$11 + 20 = 31$ $1 + 2 + 4 +$
          $8 + 16 = 31$

$100 - 69 = 31$ $31 \div 1 = 31$
$90 - 59 = 31$ $62 \div 2 = 31$
$40 - 9 = 31$ $93 \div 3 = 31$

32

$30 + 2 = 32$

$31 + 1 = 32$

$16 + 16 = 32$

$5 + 11 +$

$7 + 9 = 32$

$5 + 7 +$

$9 + 11 = 32$

$2 \times 16 = 32$

$4 \times 8 = 32$

$2 \times 2 \times 8 = 32$

$2 \times 2 \times 2 \times 4 = 32$

$2 \times 2 \times$

$2 \times 2 \times 2 = 32$

$100 - 68 = 32$

$40 - 8 = 32$

$64 - 32 = 32$

$48 - 16 = 32$

$56 - 24 = 32$

$8 \times 8 \div 2 = 32$

$6 \times 16 \div 3 = 32$

$10 + 6 + 14 + 2 = 32$

$2 + 6 + 10 + 14 = 32$

$16 \div 2 \times 4 = 32$

33

$30 + 3 = 33$

$32 + 1 = 33$

$40 - 7 = 33$

$100 - 67 = 33$

$90 - 57 = 33$

$3 \times 11 = 33$

$10 + 11 + 12 = 33$

$9 + 11 + 13 = 33$

$1 + 11 + 21 = 33$

$11 + 22 = 33$

$3 + 4 + 5 + 6 +$

$7 + 8 = 33$

$99 - 66 = 33$

$88 - 55 = 33$

$77 - 44 = 33$

$66 - 33 = 33$

$55 - 22 = 33$

$3 + 8 + 4 + 7 +$

$5 + 6 = 33$

$11 + 11 + 11 = 33$

$99 \div 3 = 33$

$99 - 33 - 33 = 33$

34

$$30 + 4 = 34 \qquad 2 \times 17 = 34$$
$$33 + 1 = 34 \qquad 17 + 17 = 34$$
$$34 \times 1 = 34 \qquad 7 + 8 + 9 + 10 = 34$$
$$34 + 0 = 34 \qquad 4 + 7 + 10 + 13 = 34$$

$$100 - 66 = 34 \qquad 29 + 5 = 34$$
$$40 - 6 = 34 \qquad 28 + 6 = 34$$
$$50 - 16 = 34 \qquad 27 + 7 = 34$$
$$90 - 56 = 34 \qquad 26 + 8 = 34$$

35

$$30 + 5 = 35 \qquad 5 \times 7 = 35$$
$$34 + 1 = 35 \qquad 7 + 7 + 7 + 7 + 7 = 35$$
$$40 - 5 = 35 \qquad 9 + 8 + 7 + 6 + 5 = 35$$
$$100 - 65 = 35 \qquad 13 + 1 + 10 +$$
$$90 - 55 = 35 \qquad 4 + 7 = 35$$
$$1 + 4 + 7 +$$
$$10 + 13 = 35$$

$$5 + 5 + 5 + 5 +$$
$$5 + 5 + 5 = 35$$
$$2 + 3 + 4 + 5 +$$
$$29 + 6 = 35 \qquad 6 + 7 + 8 = 35$$
$$28 + 7 = 35 \qquad 8 + 2 + 7 + 3 +$$
$$41 - 6 = 35 \qquad 6 + 4 + 5 = 35$$
$$42 - 7 = 35 \qquad 15 + 20 = 35$$
$$49 - 14 = 35 \qquad 3 + 5 + 7 + 9 + 11 = 35$$

36

$$30 + 6 = 36 \qquad 2 \times 18 = 36$$
$$35 + 1 = 36 \qquad 3 \times 12 = 36$$
$$40 - 4 = 36 \qquad 4 \times 9 = 36$$
$$100 - 64 = 36 \qquad 6 \times 6 = 36$$
$$90 - 54 = 36 \qquad 2 \times 2 \times 3 \times 3 = 36$$

$$12 + 12 + 12 = 36 \qquad 9 + 9 + 9 + 9 = 36$$
$$11 + 12 + 13 = 36 \qquad 8 + 1 + 7 + 2 +$$
$$11 + 1 + 9 + \qquad 6 + 3 + 5 + 4 = 36$$
$$3 + 7 + 5 = 36 \qquad 1 + 2 + 3 + 4 +$$
$$1 + 3 + 5 + \qquad 5 + 6 + 7 + 8 = 36$$
$$7 + 9 + 11 = 36 \qquad 54 - 18 = 36$$
$$45 - 9 = 36 \qquad 63 - 27 = 36$$

37

$$30 + 7 = 37 \qquad 37 \times 1 = 37$$
$$36 + 1 = 37 \qquad 74 \div 2 = 37$$
$$27 + 10 = 37 \qquad 74 - 37 = 37$$

$$100 - 63 = 37 \qquad 17 + 20 = 37$$
$$90 - 53 = 37 \qquad 18 + 19 = 37$$
$$40 - 3 = 37 \qquad 20 - 2 + 20 - 1 = 37$$

38

$$30 + 8 = 38 \qquad 2 \times 19 = 38$$
$$37 + 1 = 38 \qquad 20 + 18 = 38$$
$$45 - 7 = 38 \qquad 76 - 38 = 38$$

$$100 - 62 = 38 \qquad 8 + 9 + 10 + 11 = 38$$
$$90 - 52 = 38 \qquad 5 + 8 + 11 + 14 = 38$$
$$40 - 2 = 38 \qquad 2 + 7 + 12 + 17 = 38$$

39

$$30 + 9 = 39 \qquad 3 \times 13 = 39$$
$$38 + 1 = 39 \qquad 12 + 13 + 14 = 39$$
$$40 - 1 = 39 \qquad 11 + 13 + 15 = 39$$

$$100 - 61 = 39 \qquad 45 - 6 = 39$$
$$90 - 51 = 39 \qquad 42 - 3 = 39$$
$$52 - 13 = 39 \qquad 26 + 26 - 13 = 39$$

40

$4 \times 10 = 40$ $2 \times 20 = 40$
$30 + 10 = 40$ $4 \times 10 = 40$
$10 + 10 +$ $5 \times 8 = 40$
$10 + 10 = 40$ $2 \times 2 \times 2 \times 5 = 40$
$50 - 10 = 40$ $8 \times 10 \div 2 = 40$
$100 - 60 = 40$ $16 \div 2 \times 5 = 40$
$90 - 50 = 40$

$7 + 9 +$ $8 + 8 + 8 + 8 + 8 = 40$
$11 + 13 = 40$ $6 + 7 + 8 +$
$4 + 8 +$ $9 + 10 = 40$
$12 + 16 = 40$ $2 + 5 + 8 +$
$48 - 8 = 40$ $11 + 14 = 40$
$32 + 8 = 40$ $14 + 2 + 11 + 5 + 8 = 40$
$56 - 16 = 40$ $16 + 16 + 8 = 40$
$64 - 24 = 40$ $16 + 24 = 40$

41

$40 + 1 = 41$ $41 \times 1 = 41$
$30 + 11 = 41$ $82 \div 2 = 41$
$20 + 21 = 41$ $82 - 41 = 41$

$100 - 59 = 41$ $31 + 10 = 41$
$90 - 49 = 41$ $32 + 9 = 41$
$50 - 9 = 41$ $33 + 8 = 41$

42

$$40 + 2 = 42 \qquad 2 \times 21 = 42$$
$$41 + 1 = 42 \qquad 3 \times 14 = 42$$
$$50 - 8 = 42 \qquad 6 \times 7 = 42$$
$$100 - 58 = 42 \qquad 2 \times 3 \times 7 = 42$$

$$13 + 14 + 15 = 42$$
$$7 + 14 + 21 = 42$$
$$9 + 10 + \qquad\qquad 35 + 7 = 42$$
$$11 + 12 = 42 \qquad 28 + 14 = 42$$
$$6 + 9 + \qquad\qquad 49 - 7 = 42$$
$$12 + 15 = 42 \qquad 56 - 14 = 42$$

43

$$40 + 3 = 43 \qquad 43 \times 1 = 43$$
$$42 + 1 = 43 \qquad 86 \div 2 = 43$$
$$33 + 10 = 43 \qquad 86 - 43 = 43$$

$$100 - 57 = 43 \qquad 23 + 20 = 43$$
$$90 - 47 = 43 \qquad 13 + 30 = 43$$
$$50 - 7 = 43 \qquad 21 + 22 = 43$$

44

$40 + 4 = 44$

$43 + 1 = 44$

$100 - 56 = 44$

$50 - 6 = 44$

$2 \times 22 = 44$

$4 \times 11 = 44$

$2 \times 2 \times 11 = 44$

$8 \times 11 \div 2 = 44$

$22 + 22 = 44$

$8 + 10 + 12 + 14 = 44$

$99 - 55 = 44$

$88 - 44 = 44$

$9 + 8 + 7 + 6 +$

$77 - 33 = 44$

$5 + 4 + 3 + 2 = 44$

$66 - 22 = 44$

$45 - 1 = 44$

45

$40 + 5 = 45$

$44 + 1 = 45$

$90 - 45 = 45$

$100 - 55 = 45$

$50 - 5 = 45$

$3 \times 15 = 45$

$5 \times 9 = 45$

$3 \times 3 \times 5 = 45$

$9 \times 10 \div 2 = 45$

$6 \times 15 \div 2 = 45$

$1 + 2 + 3 + 4 + 5 +$

$6 + 7 + 8 + 9 = 45$

$15 + 15 + 15 = 45$

$75 - 30 = 45$

$5 + 15 + 25 = 45$

$60 - 15 = 45$

$7 + 8 + 9 +$

$54 - 9 = 45$

$10 + 11 = 45$

$63 - 18 = 45$

$5 + 7 + 9 +$

$72 - 27 = 45$

$11 + 13 = 45$

222 •

46

40 + 6 = 46   2 × 23 = 46
45 + 1 = 46   23 + 23 = 46
50 − 4 = 46   69 − 23 = 46

100 − 54 = 46   10 + 11 + 12 + 13 = 46
90 − 44 = 46   1 + 8 + 15 + 22 = 46
60 − 14 = 46   30 + 16 = 46

47

40 + 7 = 47   47 × 1 = 47
46 + 1 = 47   94 ÷ 2 = 47
45 + 2 = 47   94 − 47 = 47

100 − 53 = 47   37 + 10 = 47
90 − 43 = 47   27 + 20 = 47
50 − 3 = 47   17 + 30 = 47

48

40 + 8 = 48	2 × 24 = 48
47 + 1 = 48	3 × 16 = 48
50 − 2 = 48	4 × 12 = 48
90 − 42 = 48	6 × 8 = 48
100 − 52 = 48	2 × 2 × 2 × 2 × 3 = 48
	12 + 12 + 12 + 12 = 48
16 + 16 + 16 = 48	9 + 11 + 13 + 15 = 48
8 + 16 + 24 = 48	3 + 9 + 15 + 21 = 48
56 − 8 = 48	8 + 8 + 8 + 8 + 8 + 8 = 48
72 − 24 = 48	3 + 5 + 7 + 9 + 11 + 13 = 48
96 − 48 = 48	

49

40 + 9 = 49	7 × 7 = 49
48 + 1 = 49	7 + 7 + 7 + 7 + 7 + 7 + 7 = 49
50 − 1 = 49	1 + 3 + 5 + 7 + 9 + 11 + 13 = 49
100 − 51 = 49	4 + 5 + 6 + 7 + 8 + 9 + 10 = 49
56 − 7 = 49	7 + 42 = 49
63 − 14 = 49	14 + 35 = 49
70 − 21 = 49	21 + 28 = 49
98 − 49 = 49	77 − 28 = 49

50

$$5 \times 10 = 50 \qquad 2 \times 25 = 50$$
$$49 + 1 = 50 \qquad 5 \times 10 = 50$$
$$100 - 50 = 50 \qquad 2 \times 5 \times 5 = 50$$
$$90 - 40 = 50 \qquad 15 \times 5 \div 3 \times 2 = 50$$

$$10 + 10 + 10 +$$
$$10 + 10 = 50$$
$$8 + 9 + 10 +$$
$$10 + 40 = 50 \qquad 11 + 12 = 50$$
$$20 + 30 = 50 \qquad 6 + 8 + 10 +$$
$$5 + 10 + \qquad 12 + 14 = 50$$
$$15 + 20 = 50 \qquad 11 + 12 +$$
$$10 \times 10 \div 2 = 50 \qquad 13 + 14 = 50$$

51

$$50 + 1 = 51 \qquad 3 \times 17 = 51$$
$$41 + 10 = 51 \qquad 17 + 17 + 17 = 51$$
$$31 + 20 = 51 \qquad 16 + 17 + 18 = 51$$

$$100 - 49 = 51 \qquad 21 + 30 = 51$$
$$90 - 39 = 51 \qquad 11 + 40 = 51$$
$$60 - 9 = 51 \qquad 15 + 17 + 19 = 51$$

52

$$50 + 2 = 52 \qquad 2 \times 26 = 52$$
$$51 + 1 = 52 \qquad 4 \times 13 = 52$$
$$60 - 8 = 52 \qquad 2 \times 2 \times 13 = 52$$

$$100 - 48 = 52 \qquad 10 + 12 + 14 + 16 = 52$$
$$26 + 26 = 52 \qquad 1 + 9 + 17 + 25 = 52$$
$$13 + 39 = 52 \qquad 13 + 13 + 13 + 13 = 52$$

53

$$50 + 3 = 53 \qquad 53 \times 1 = 53$$
$$52 + 1 = 53 \qquad 33 + 20 = 53$$
$$43 + 10 = 53 \qquad 23 + 30 = 53$$

$$100 - 47 = 53 \qquad 13 + 40 = 53$$
$$90 - 37 = 53 \qquad 45 + 8 = 53$$
$$60 - 7 = 53 \qquad 53 + 0 = 53$$

54

$50 + 4 = 54$
$53 + 1 = 54$
$60 - 6 = 54$
$100 - 46 = 54$
$75 - 21 = 54$

$2 \times 27 = 54$
$3 \times 18 = 54$
$6 \times 9 = 54$
$2 \times 3 \times 3 \times 3 = 54$
$9 + 9 + 9 + 9 + 9 + 9 = 54$

$12 + 13 + 14 + 15 = 54$

$63 - 9 = 54$
$72 - 18 = 54$
$81 - 27 = 54$
$90 - 36 = 54$
$45 + 9 = 54$

$9 + 12 + 15 + 18 = 54$
$17 + 18 + 19 = 54$
$9 + 18 + 27 = 54$
$4 + 6 + 8 + 10 + 12 + 14 = 54$

55

$50 + 5 = 55$
$54 + 1 = 55$
$60 - 5 = 55$
$100 - 45 = 55$
$90 - 35 = 55$

$5 \times 11 = 55$
$11 + 11 + 11 + 11 + 11 = 55$
$9 + 10 + 11 + 12 + 13 = 55$
$7 + 9 + 11 + 13 + 15 = 55$
$15 + 7 + 13 + 9 + 11 = 55$

$99 - 44 = 55$
$88 - 33 = 55$
$77 - 22 = 55$
$66 - 11 = 55$
$55 - 0 = 55$

$3 + 7 + 11 + 15 + 19 = 55$
$19 + 3 + 15 + 7 + 11 = 55$
$22 + 22 + 11 = 55$
$44 + 11 = 55$
$33 + 22 = 55$

56

$50 + 6 = 56$

$55 + 1 = 56$

$60 - 4 = 56$

$100 - 44 = 56$

$90 - 34 = 56$

$63 - 7 = 56$

$2 \times 28 = 56$

$4 \times 14 = 56$

$7 \times 8 = 56$

$8 \times 7 = 56$

$2 \times 2 \times 2 \times 7 = 56$

$6 \times 7 \div 3 \times 4 = 56$

$2 + 4 + 6 + 8 +$
$10 + 12 + 14 = 56$

$5 + 6 + 7 + 8 +$

$70 - 14 = 56$

$9 + 10 + 11 = 56$

$77 - 21 = 56$

$11 + 5 + 10 + 6 +$

$64 - 8 = 56$

$9 + 7 + 8 = 56$

$72 - 16 = 56$

$16 + 16 + 16 + 8 = 56$

$80 - 24 = 56$

$11 + 13 + 15 + 17 = 56$

$88 - 32 = 56$

$8 + 12 + 16 + 20 = 56$

57

$50 + 7 = 57$

$56 + 1 = 57$

$60 - 3 = 57$

$100 - 43 = 57$

$3 \times 19 = 57$

$95 \div 5 \times 3 = 57$

$19 + 19 + 19 = 57$

$20 + 20 + 20 - 3 = 57$

$76 - 19 = 57$

$95 - 38 = 57$

$38 + 19 = 57$

$40 + 20 - 3 = 57$

$18 + 19 + 20 = 57$

$17 + 19 + 21 = 57$

$16 + 19 + 22 = 57$

$15 + 19 + 23 = 57$

58

$50 + 8 = 58$

$57 + 1 = 58$

$48 + 10 = 58$

$2 \times 29 = 58$

$29 + 29 = 58$

$1 + 10 + 19 + 28 = 58$

$100 - 42 = 58$

$90 - 32 = 58$

$60 - 2 = 58$

$13 + 14 + 15 + 16 = 58$

$10 + 13 + 16 + 19 = 58$

$7 + 12 + 17 + 22 = 58$

59

$50 + 9 = 59$

$58 + 1 = 59$

$59 \times 1 = 59$

$60 - 1 = 59$

$100 - 41 = 59$

$90 - 31 = 59$

$49 + 10 = 59$

$39 + 20 = 59$

60

$6 \times 10 = 60$ $2 \times 30 = 60$

$59 + 1 = 60$ $3 \times 20 = 60$

$100 - 40 = 60$ $4 \times 15 = 60$

$90 - 30 = 60$ $5 \times 12 = 60$

$75 - 15 = 60$ $6 \times 10 = 60$

$45 + 15 = 60$ $2 \times 2 \times 3 \times 5 = 60$

$50 + 10 = 60$ $3 \times 4 \times 5 = 60$

$5 + 7 + 9 + 11 +$

$54 + 6 = 60$ $13 + 15 = 60$

$48 + 12 = 60$ $10 + 11 + 12 + 13 + 14 = 60$

$42 + 18 = 60$ $4 + 8 + 12 + 16 + 20 = 60$

$36 + 24 = 60$ $12 + 14 + 16 + 18 = 60$

$66 - 6 = 60$ $6 + 12 + 18 + 24 = 60$

$72 - 12 = 60$ $19 + 20 + 21 = 60$

$84 - 24 = 60$ $10 + 20 + 30 = 60$

More Information About How to Teach Your Child

The Gentle Revolution Encyclopedic Knowledge Series includes the following *Bit of Intelligence* Sets:

A R T

Great Art Masterpieces
Self-Portraits of Great Artists
Masterpieces by da Vinci
Masterpieces by Picasso
Masterpieces by van Gogh

NATURAL HISTORY

Amphibians – Set I   Flowers
Primates – Set I   Insects
Birds   Leaves
Birds of Prey   Mammals
Butterflies and Moths   Reptiles
Dinosaurs   Sea Creatures

PEOPLE

Composers   Great Inventors
Explorers   World Leaders
Presidents of the United States – Set I

FOREIGN LANGUAGE

Basic Vocabulary in 10 Languages

MUSIC

Musical Instruments

ANATOMY

Organs of the Body

MATHEMATICS

Regular Polygons

PICTURE DICTIONARY
CD-ROMS

The Gentle Revolution Series includes ten volumes of the *Picture Dictionary CD-ROMs.*

The Picture Dictionary Program is designed to give parents a very easy-to-use method of introducing a program of encyclopedic knowledge in five different languages. A child may concentrate on a favorite language or gain ability in all five languages.

Each CD-ROM contains fifteen categories of Bit of Intelligence images, with ten images in each category. That is a total of 150 different images that can be viewed in English, Spanish, Japanese, Italian, and French on each CD-ROM.

For each image there is a large reading word provided. The child may choose to view the image and the reading word, the image alone, or the reading word alone. Mother and child may also create their own category by choosing images from the 150 images available on each CD-ROM.

This program is so easy to navigate that children as young as three years old have been able to use it independently.

RELATED BOOKS, VIDEOS & KITS
IN THE GENTLE REVOLUTION SERIES

HOW TO TEACH YOUR BABY TO READ
Glenn Doman and Janet Doman

How To Teach Your Baby To Read provides your child with the enjoyment of reading. It shows you just how easy and pleasurable it is to teach a young child to read. It explains how to begin and expand the reading program, how to make and organize your materials, and how to more fully develop your child's potential.

Also available: **How To Teach Your Baby To Read™ Video**
                       How To Teach Your Baby To Read™ Kits

HOW TO TEACH YOUR BABY MATH
Glenn Doman and Janet Doman

How To Teach Your Baby Math instructs you in successfully developing your child's ability to think and reason. It shows you just how easy and pleasurable it is to teach a young child math. It explains how to begin and expand the math program, how to make and organize your materials, and how to more fully develop your child's potential.

Also available: **How To Teach Your Baby Math™ Video**
                       How To Teach Your Baby Math™ Kits

HOW TO GIVE YOUR BABY ENCYCLOPEDIC KNOWLEDGE
Glenn Doman, Janet Doman, and Susan Aisen

How To Give Your Baby Encyclopedic Knowledge provides a program of visually stimulating information designed to help your child take advantage of his or her natural potential to learn anything. It shows you just how easy and pleasurable it is to teach a young child about the arts, science, and nature. Your child will recognize the insects in the garden, know the countries of the world, discover the beauty of a painting by van Gogh, and more. It explains how to begin and expand your program, how to make and organize your materials, and how to more fully develop your child's potential.

Also available: **How To Give Your Baby Encyclopedic Knowledge™ Video**
How To Give Your Baby Encyclopedic Knowledge™ Kits

HOW TO MULTIPLY YOUR BABY'S INTELLIGENCE
Glenn Doman and Janet Doman

How To Multiply Your Baby's Intelligence provides a comprehensive program that will enable your child to read, to do mathematics, and to learn about anything and everything. It shows you just how easy and pleasurable it is to teach your young child, and to help your child become more capable and confident. It explains how to begin and expand this remarkable program, how to make and organize your materials, and how to more fully develop your child's potential.

Also available: **How To Multiply Your Baby's Intelligence™ Kits**

HOW TO TEACH YOUR BABY TO BE PHYSICALLY SUPERB
Glenn Doman, Douglas Doman, and Bruce Hagy

How To Teach Your Baby To Be Physically Superb explains the basic principles, philosophy, and stages of mobility in easy-to-understand language. This inspiring book describes just how easy and pleasurable it is to teach a young child to be physically superb. It clearly shows you how to create an environment for each stage of mobility that will help your baby advance and develop more easily. It shows that the team of mother, father, and baby is the most important athletic team your child will ever know. It explains how to begin, how to make your materials, and how to expand your program. This complete guide also includes full-color charts, photographs, illustrations, and detailed instructions to help you create your own program.

Also available: **How To Teach Your Baby To Be Physically Superb™ Video**

WHAT TO DO ABOUT YOUR BRAIN-INJURED CHILD
Glenn Doman

In this breakthrough book, Glenn Doman—pioneer in the treatment of the brain-injured—brings real hope to thousands of children, many of whom are inoperable, and many of whom have been given up for lost and sentenced to a life of institutional confinement. Based upon the decades of successful work performed at The Institutes for the Achievement of Human Potential, the book explains why old theories and techniques fail, and why The Institutes philosophy and revolutionary treatment succeed.

CHILDREN'S BOOKS
About the Books

Very young readers have special needs. These are not met
by conventional children's literature, which is designed to
be read by adults to little children, not by them. The careful choice of vocabulary, sentence structure, print size, and
formatting is needed by very young readers. The design of
these children's books is based upon almost a half-century
of search and discovery of what works best for very young
readers.

ENOUGH, INIGO, ENOUGH
written by Janet Doman, illustrated by Michael Armentrout
Ages 1 to 6

NOSE IS NOT TOES
written by Glenn Doman, illustrated by Janet Doman
Ages 1 to 3

COURSES
offered at The Institutes for the Achievement of Human Potential

HOW TO MULTIPLY YOUR BABY'S INTELLIGENCE™ COURSE

WHAT TO DO ABOUT YOUR BRAIN-INJURED CHILD™ COURSE

For course and program information,
please contact:

The Institutes for the Achievement of Human Potential
8801 Stenton Avenue
Wyndmoor, PA 19038 USA

www.iahp.org

PHONE: 215-233-2050
FAX: 215-233-3940

For books and teaching materials,
please contact:

The Gentle Revolution Press
810 Gleneagles Court, Suite 305
Towson, MD 21286 USA

www.gentlerevolution.com

TOLL-FREE PHONE: 866-250-BABY
FAX: 410-337-3544

Index